ADHD! What's Next?

Parenting Solutions
for Home and School

Eric Unruh, MSW, LCSW
Gary Unruh, MSW, LCSW

Lighthouse Love Productions, LLC
COLORADO SPRINGS, CO

First printing 2017
ISBN 978-0-9824204-2-3

ATTENTION CORPORATIONS, UNIVERSITIES, COLLEGES,
AND PROFESSIONAL ORGANIZATIONS: Quantity discounts are available
on bulk purchases of this booklet for educational, gift purposes, or as premiums
for increasing magazine subscriptions or renewals. Special books or
book excerpts can also be created to fit specific needs.
For information, please contact Lighthouse Love Productions, LLC,
7680 Goddard Street, Suite 215, Colorado Springs, CO 80920;

ADHDParentingSolutions.com

TABLE OF CONTENTS

Section One: Understanding ADHD

Section Two: My Child Has ADHD—Now What?

INSIDE THE MIND of a child with ADHD: "I need to get started on my work, but I just can't get myself to do it... It's boring... I can't keep my mind on it... I waited too long... This is going to take way more time than I thought... I'm rushing... Oh no, I forgot my worksheet I needed... I'm so far behind now... My parents are going to be so upset... I do this to myself all the time... Why can't I figure this out?... WHAT'S MY PROBLEM?!"

Inside the mind of a parent with an ADHD child: "Why wasn't this done?... I gave plenty of reminders... Why are you angry at me?... I'm just trying to help... It's always an argument or broken promise... Things never seem to get finished without a fight... Can't you try harder?... Why don't you listen to me the first time?... How are you going to make it without me helping you?... What am I doing wrong as a parent?... Why can't I get my child to do this?... WHAT'S MY PROBLEM?!"

Authors GARY and ERIC UNRUH understand those thoughts. They are not only professionals with over 60 years combined experience counseling children with ADHD and their families, but they have ADHD themselves. They have faced their own personal challenges, but more importantly, successes with ADHD. They understand what it's like for a child with ADHD, and what it's like for their parents. They get it, because they have lived it.

Many children and adults struggle for years, not realizing they even have ADHD. Actually, many live their entire life without knowing. Being identified as having ADHD isn't a bad thing. It's actually life changing. There is a shift of thought from "What's my problem?" to "Oh... that's what's been going on!" Knowing that it's ADHD brings clarity, offers direction and gives hope.

What can a parent do to help their child living with ADHD? There are two things:

1. Gain a better understanding of what ADHD is. Section one of this book is called "Understanding ADHD" and is designed to help parents gain a better understanding of exactly what it is, and what it's like to live with ADHD.

2. Adjust their parenting technique in ways that work with children who have ADHD. Section two of this book is called "My Child Has ADHD. Now What?" and offers parenting strategies to help ADHD children successfully manage their ADHD for the rest of their lives.

There are many success stories of children with ADHD. Need an example? It is thought that Albert Einstein, Emily Dickenson, Henry Ford and Thomas Edison all had ADHD. Each one of them is considered successful. Current actor Channing Tatum and music star Justin Timberlake have disclosed they have ADHD as well. The bottom line is your child may have ADHD, but that doesn't mean they can't be successful. Your child is full of potential. By having a deeper understanding of ADHD and learning how to effectively parent an ADHD child, you can play a big role in helping your child develop into a happy, healthy and successful adult. So let's get started!

Section One:

Understanding ADHD

A Day
in the Life...

"AH-H-H-H-H-H—STOP IT!" It's 6:14 a.m. and 10-year-old Chad has awakened the household. He already pushed his little sister to the edge by throwing Lego pieces at her while she tried to sleep. Chad's mother is jolted awake by the shrieking scream and realizes it's time to clock in and get to work. There is no rest for the weary (for that matter, there isn't any rest working as a zookeeper either).

Guessing accurately that her son is provoking her 6-year-old daughter, Mom yells, "Chad, if you do that again, no TV this morning." With that threat, Chad gallops downstairs. He is full of excitement because after school his parents are taking him to the Extreme Bounce Paradise, a huge building filled with inflatable trampolines, slides and obstacle courses. It's a crazy, loud place that pushes the envelope on a kid's primal climbing and jumping abilities, while at the same time testing every inch of a parent's tolerance and patience. He can't wait.

Chad is hungry, so he very responsibly makes a bowl of cereal for himself. He completes every step in getting out the cereal, bowl, spoon, and milk. But looking forward to watching TV while he eats, he forgets to put the cereal away and clean up after himself. As he watches TV he seems to shift into a different mindset, a different mental zone. He is completely calm and focused on the show, as if his high energy from only moments ago had been switched off.

After a few minutes his mother yells, "It's time to turn off the TV and get to school."

So incredibly focused on the show, without turning Chad yells, "Not yet!" This is repeated 3 or 4 times. After more threats from his mother that he will lose privileges if he doesn't listen, he finally turns off the TV and heads for the car, but leaves his cereal bowl on the coffee table.

Before getting into the car, Chad realizes he forgot his math homework and quickly heads back into the house to get it. His mother stops him halfway and says, "Wipe up that milk you spilled this morning." Irritated and annoyed that his mother had the guts to interrupt what he was doing, he turns to the milk on the floor. He does not verbally acknowledge his mother's request, but growls instead.

Rather than taking the time to get a paper towel, he simply decides to wipe it up with his sock and proclaims, "All done."

His mother responds, "Don't forget to put away the video games and controllers you left on the floor before you leave... and your cereal bowl on the coffee table."

He shouts back, "I'll do it after school."

His mother responds, "You always say that, but it never gets done."

He yells, "Whatever! That's not true. I will this time, now let's go—we are late," and runs back to the car. Unfortunately, because he got sidetracked wiping up spilled milk and listening to the other requests, he forgets the math homework he originally went back to pick up.

Now in the car on their way to school, he finds the drive 100% boring. Chad can't stand having nothing to do. To make things less boring he decides to add some spice to the situation and starts to irritate his sister again by flicking her hair. He has a quota to make his sister angry at least 10 times in one day, you know. This makes his sister yell, which makes him laugh. In the chaos his mother thinks, *I wonder what is considered more dangerous—driving while texting or driving with kids yelling in the back seat of the car?* Again, she has to make a threat. "If you keep this up, you will not be going to the Extreme Bounce Paradise after school today." Like her other threats, this gets his attention and works like a charm. Mom thinks to herself, *Why do I always need to threaten him to make him behave? It shouldn't be this way.*

Chad's mother remembers that she finished proof reading his short paper for English class last night, so she tells him, "Hey, I was able to look over your paper last night and there are just a few corrections you will need to make tonight when you get home."

In frustration Chad responds, "Why do I have to make corrections? Isn't it good enough as it is?" Chad hates being told to do things again, especially when he hated doing it the first time around. He grumbles, "I might correct it, I might not…depends how I feel." Right then his eyes roll upward as he tries to mentally calculate his current grade in English to see if he really needs to make the corrections or not. If this current paper doesn't matter to hold his current "C" in that subject, then he figures he doesn't need to do it. He also knows it is only the first month of school, and there is plenty of time to get his grade up later in the semester if he really needs to.

They arrive at school and he jumps out of the car, so hurried that he doesn't shut the car door completely. His mother yells out, "Shut the door," but to no avail. He is already gone to find his friends. In his pocket he brought a collection of some of his best Pokémon cards to show off. For some reason when it comes to his Pokémon cards he is able to focus very well on remembering all the information on the cards and is very good at keeping them organized and together. He is also very good at not losing them or forgetting them. *Why can't he be that way with his school work?* his mom wonders.

As Mom drives out of the school parking lot, she feels some relief to have a break from all the noise and tension of the morning. This relaxed feeling quickly starts to change as sadness suddenly rushes in. She thinks back and realizes most of her interactions with Chad that morning seemed negative, as they do most mornings. She wishes she had more positive interactions with him, but she feels much of her time with Chad is spent modifying his behavior which only seems to make Chad angry at her. She wonders if she is being a good parent or doing something wrong. This certainly isn't the way she pictured things with her son.

Chad daydreams throughout the entire school day about how much fun he will have at the Extreme Bounce Paradise and he can't get his mind off it. This makes it more difficult to focus on what is going on in class. His friend will be meeting him there after school, but unlike Chad, his friend is able to push the excitement aside and focus on what the teacher is saying. As the teacher gives instructions, Chad finds some of what she is saying interesting and during these times he finds it easier to pay attention. But for the other less interesting stuff, he finds that his mind wanders and gravitates to other things. As the words of his teacher start to drift from his awareness, he suddenly hears a jet flying by and looks out the window into the sky in an attempt to identify what kind of airplane it is. He loves jets and is very sharp at being able to quickly identify what kind of jet it is. In fact, he is quite observant and knowledgeable about many things.

Chad starts tipping his chair back onto two legs when his teacher isn't looking. He enjoys the challenge of balancing on the chair's two back legs, as the act of balancing like this requires focus and precision. He tries to see if he can break yesterday's "2 leg balance record" set at 7.3 seconds. It's much more interesting than the current science class subject of evaporation. His chair starts bumping into another student who assertively whispers, "Stop, that's annoying!" Without warning, Chad tips just a little too far back in the chair and falls to the floor with a crash. The kids laugh and the teacher looks at him and says, "Chad I've told you not to do that." Embarrassed and more serious now, he grabs the worksheet the class is working on, but quickly starts to lose interest again. He begins to draw instead, something between a spider and teacher, naming it "Speacher."

Suddenly Chad realizes the teacher is talking about what page to start on with their math assignment. He perks up to listen so he doesn't miss it and quickly thinks to himself, *Got it!* before she is finished giving the instructions. He tries hard to focus on getting his math work done, but he is soon distracted. His ears seem to pick up every noise in the class—the clock ticking, the teacher making non-rhythmic taps on her keyboard, the kids in the hallway, and the really strange whistling sounds coming out of that kid's nose sitting behind him. Out of the corner of his eye he notices every movement in the room, like the kid beside him flapping his pencil back and forth, the teacher getting up from her desk and "HEY GUYS LOOK—two fighter jets in formation in the sky just like last Tuesday!" Even sensations can distract him, like tags in his shirt or socks that don't feel right on his toes. These various inputs to the brain seem to enter his awareness all at the same time, as if his brain is on high alert and allowing every sight, sound and sensation through the flood gate all at once.

He lightly hits his forehead with the palm of his hand, as if to shake out the distractions. He quietly says to himself, *Come on, think... think!* It's funny he is having such problems getting the math work done because he is a very smart kid, especially in math. Strangely enough, it seems the easier and less challenging the math questions are, the harder it is for Chad to focus on the work and block out the distractions. For some of the questions he thinks, *This is too easy. I know these. What's the point?*

With two or three times more effort than it took most of the other kids in class, he finally finishes the assignment. Chad completed every problem on the page assigned by his teacher, BUT unfortunately he had not heard her say they only had to do the even-numbered problems. This frustrates him. He did more work than was required, and doing more than expected is definitely NOT his style.

The teacher then asks the class to turn in their math homework from yesterday. He digs through his backpack that looks more like a trash can, and realizes he left it in his room (the trash dump). At the end of class the teacher posts current grades and he notices he is failing math now. Getting a "C" is fine, a "D" concerns him, but an "F" is trouble. He starts to feel frustrated, but also nervous and anxious. He feels he is really trying but can't seem to get good grades. He figures he will keep the bad grade to himself so he can still go to the Bounce place. Little does he know, his teacher has already sounded the alarm to his parents by engaging the Emergency "You're Busted" Email System (or the EYBES). Kids hate it.

As his mother parks her car at school to pick the kids up, she gets an alert sound on her cell phone that a new email from Chad's math teacher has arrived. In the email the teacher writes, "Hey, I just wanted to express my concerns to you about how Chad isn't turning in all of his work and it is affecting his grade." His mom reads a statement that she has heard maybe 2 or maybe 83 times before: "He is very capable and smart with lots of potential. If he would just put his mind to his work and try, he could be doing much better." Chad's mom agrees, but wonders how she can make him "put his mind to it" or "try." If it were that easy, it would have already happened.

Just as she finishes reading the email, the doors open and the kids jump into the car. She figures she will mention the email later, in order to have some positive interaction with the kids. "How was your day?" she asks.

Chad's sister responds, "Great! We had a guest speaker come and talk about owls."

Then it's Chad's turn. In a frustrated tone he tells her, "Don't ask."

"Okay, sounds like a typical day," Mom replies. Trying to lift Chad's mood, she says excitedly, "Let's go to the Extreme Bounce Paradise!"

When they arrive, Chad acts just like every other kid by going down the inflatable slides and jumping on the inflatable trampoline

But after a little while he decides he needs more excitement and it's time to up the ante. He climbs on top of the bounce house, which is not permitted. He yells to his friends to look at him as his head is almost touching the roof of the building. He looks like some sort of wild creature, and if it weren't so dangerous, you would have to give the kid some credit for finding a way to get up that high where "no man or kid has ever been before." He laughs and the other kids also find him very amusing, so he starts to dance a jig. That makes the other kids laugh even harder. He doesn't see the harm in doing this and thoroughly enjoys entertaining his audience. His mother sees him and yells at him to get down. He defies her at first, but after threats of grounding him, he finally climbs down. His mother feels embarrassed that all the other parents were witness to the show. She wonders to herself if today will be the day she finally loses her mind.

Back at home, the family sits down to have dinner together. Chad is very fun to talk with and very amusing. He loves his family and even loves—well, likes—his little sister. Before long he has them all laughing hard as he starts doing his classic imitations and making jokes. He is very engaging socially and others really enjoy his energy and personality. He really likes these moments with his family, especially when they are not talking about chores or schoolwork.

After dinner his parents kindly remind him to get started on what he thinks is one of the worst things in the world: homework. This is met with significant resistance and Chad's parents have to once again threaten to take away privileges if he does not do his homework. His mother reminds him, "Remember that paper I talked to you about this morning, and how I made corrections and you said..."

Quickly interrupting and finishing her sentence, Chad responds, "I know, I know. I need to fix my paper." Chad hates it when he knows what others are going to say and don't just get to the point (especially his parents). If they don't get to the point, he will finish what they are saying and get to the point for them.

After 30 minutes of stalling and arguing, he finally starts his homework. His parents say to each other, "It took him longer to argue about the homework than it did to just get it done." This happens almost every night. He thinks he is finished with his homework, but then realizes he didn't bring home his spelling words. He thinks, *I'll review them right before class and wing it.* Unfortunately that has never worked, and as the evening comes to a close, both Chad and his parents feel frustrated and discouraged.

Chad's parents have a discussion later that night. Something needs to change. Chad is not making progress, and they fear things are actually getting worse. They are trying so hard with their child, but it seems they are only met with resistance. They are devoting 50% or more of their attention on him and wonder if their other 2 children are suffering from it.

Chad lays in his bed thinking how boring and frustrating school is, how he is failing his classes, and worries about how he will make it through school another week. Even worse, it's only Monday and he has four more days of school this week. He feels the only thing he and his parents talk about are his poor, failing grades. The grades have started to define him. Not only is he getting failing grades, he is starting to think, *I AM a failure. I might as well give up.* Little does he know, his parents feel just as discouraged and wonder, *What else can we do that we haven't already done?* His parents are good parents, but it seems nothing is working.

Does this story sound familiar? It sounds like a complicated day this child and his family made it through, doesn't it? Some of you reading this may be amazed at how familiar this story sounds. Regardless, this is a fairly typical day for an ADHD child and family. It is not easy.

Nothing Is "Wrong" with an ADHD Person

THERE ISN'T NECESSARILY anything "wrong" or "broken" with somebody diagnosed with Attention Deficit Hyperactivity Disorder (ADHD). It is more of a *description* of a person, describing *part* of the makeup of who they are and how they behave. This description doesn't need to be labeled "good" or "bad." There is a mix of positive and problematical qualities in an ADHD person, just as there is with any other person. The category of ADHD is simply describing some of the traits of a person.

ADHD is classified as a "disorder," but what is considered *disordered* is only relevant based on the particular setting a person is in. The ADHD student who is expected to sit still in a chair for five or six hours a day listening to the teacher's lectures may look more disordered in that setting. But the same child in another setting may not look at all disordered.

Here is an example. Consider a ten-year-old girl who has ADHD. She was participating in a parade and was given the job to hand out candy to all the kids along the parade route. She was running around like crazy doing her assigned task, and yelling, "I'm on a mission to make sure I give candy to every kid on the street today!" She looked like a graceful humming bird, quickly going from flower to flower.

She was doing a great job. She looked "normal" in that setting. In fact, she wasn't just normal—she was extremely helpful and energetic in accomplishing her goal. On the other hand, if this same child was in a classroom and had issues staying in her chair and focusing on her work, she may look like she has a disorder. What is "disordered" and "normal" really depends on the child's setting.

ADHD by
the Numbers

AS THE YEARS go by, we are starting to better understand ADHD. Studies show an increased number of students diagnosed with ADHD. The American Psychiatric Association states in the Diagnostic and Statistical Manual of Mental Disorders (DSM-5) that 1 out of 20 school-aged children have ADHD[1]. Some studies suggest higher rates. There are more boys than girls diagnosed with ADHD, however, girls who have ADHD are often missed because they tend to be less hyperactive or disruptive. Since a genetic link with ADHD has been discovered, often one of the parents is also ADHD. If your child is diagnosed, it might be worth reflecting on whether or not you have ADHD.

There are certain conditions that have a higher chance of co-occurring with ADHD.

- Learning disabilities (commonly co-occur[1])
- Tourette's syndrome or other tic disorders (may co-occur[1])
- Conduct disorder (25 % chance[1])
- Oppositional defiant disorder (50% chance[1])
- Anxiety disorders (Slight increased chance[1])
- Obsessive compulsive disorder (may co-occur[1])

- Depression (Slight increased chance[1])
- Bipolar or mood dysregulation disorder (The DSM-5 specifically states, "Most children and adolescents with disruptive mood dysregulation disorder have symptoms that also meet criteria for ADHD; a lesser percentage of children with ADHD have symptoms that meet criteria for disruptive new dysregulation disorder."[1])
- Autism (may co-occur[1])
- Substance abuse disorder (slight increased chance[1])

There are also conditions that mimic or look like ADHD, but *may* not be:

- Reactive attachment disorder
- Issues with blood sugar levels, such as hypoglycemia
- Issues related to blood flow, such as hypotension
- Issues with hearing and/or vision
- Tic disorders such as Tourette's (also mentioned above as related conditions)
- Substance abuse
- Nutrition deficits (such as iron deficiency)
- Reactions caused by food allergies or sensitivities
- Deficits with intellectual developmental
- Environmental exposure to toxins such as lead (The DSM-5 reports there is no evidence yet of causation between environmental toxins and developing ADHD)
- Neurological disorders such as seizure disorders
- Sleep disorders
- Sensory integration issues
- Side effects from medications
- Thyroid issues

- Gifted intellectual abilities
- Environmental stressors (such as death of a loved one or conflicts at home)
- Psychotic disorders

For some reason, there continues to be a great deal of dispute on just how many kids have ADHD. Some feel that ADHD is over-diagnosed and some feel it isn't. Regardless, ADHD is NOT over-diagnosed by those who specialize in ADHD and take the time to gather clinical information to make an accurate assessment. If a child clearly meets the clinical criteria set in the DSM-5 for ADHD, they have ADHD. It's not really productive to dispute over-diagnosis or under-diagnosis of ADHD. If a child has it, they have it, and if they don't, they don't.

---

1 *Diagnostic and Statistical Manual of Mental Disorders*, 5th Edition (DMS-5). American Psychiatric Association, Arlington, VA; 2013.

The Classic
Definition Is Misleading

THE CLASSIC DEFINITION of ADHD is found in the *Diagnostic and Statistical Manual of Mental Disorders* (DSM-5). It breaks down ADHD into 3 types:

- ADHD Predominately Inattentive Presentation (often referred to as ADD)
- ADHD—Predominately Hyperactive/Impulsive Presentation
- ADHD—Combined Presentation (Both Inattentive and Hyperactive/Impulsive Presentations.

The severity of the ADHD symptoms are then defined as severe, moderate, or mild. There is also an option to diagnose the ADHD in partial remission.

These three diagnosis categories have been used for years. Attention Deficit Hyperactivity Disorder is the last of three previous labels assigned to ADHD in the Diagnostic and Statistical Manual of Mental Disorder (DSM). It's hard to believe, but before 1968 ADHD was commonly referred to as "minimal brain dysfunction." In 1968, (DSM-II) it was referred to as Hyperkinetic Reaction of Childhood; in 1980, (DSM-III) it was Attention-Deficit, ADD; and in 1987 (DSM-III- R) it was labeled Attention-Deficit Hyperactivity Disorder. Each of these labels is misleading. Based on the diagnosis name, you may think it's only about being "hyperactive," "impulsive," "inattentive," and nothing more. Truthfully, many normally developing children are at least somewhat hyperactive, impulsive, and/or inattentive. Inattention, hyperactivity, and impulsivity are only a few of the symptoms of ADHD, but there are many more which are described in this book. The diagnosis name itself is due for a change, as it is misleading as to what ADHD really is.

What is ADHD, Really?

THE FOLLOWING SECTIONS break down what ADHD is, in real-life terms (not clinical). Keep in mind, the ADHD descriptions and symptoms below are things we all experience to some extent or at some point in our lives. The difference in ADHD children is that these symptoms are (1) constant, (2) regular in all settings (like home and school), and (3) cause significant disruption and impairment in those settings. When the three criteria are observed, a trained professional that specializes in ADHD is recommended to make an official ADHD diagnosis. Here are the typical traits you will find with an ADHD child.

ADHD kids are too attentive, not "attention deficit." The term "attention deficit" is within the diagnosis name itself. It seems to imply that the ADHD person is just blank or empty of thought. But, is the ADHD child really attention deficit?

The answer is *no*—they are actually *too attentive* to what is interesting to them and *way too attentive* to things going on around them. This may lead to problems regulating what they *need* or *should* be paying attention to. Just saying they are "inattentive" doesn't describe the core of the problem at all. This is a very different way of thinking about ADHD.

Their minds are not inattentive, but in reality, open and striving to be stimulated. Ideas and thoughts run through their mind at a much higher rate than people without ADHD. Unfortunately, at times this can be overwhelming. Sounds, sensations and sights can flow into an ADHD child's mind all at once.

Imagine you are at a boring training seminar. While the speaker gives his presentation, there are multiple flashing lights on the right side of the stage, a loud stereo blaring on the left side of the stage, a large HDTV behind the presenter showing the "20 Most Outrageously Funny Cat Videos Of All Time," and somebody behind you continually kicking your chair. Now, what did the presenter say? Welcome to the world of an ADHD child. Kids with ADHD may be overly distracted by noises outside the classroom, a tag on their t-shirt, or people moving around in class. It is as if their brain just will not say "no, I'm not letting you in" and is sucking in all the information at once. They are *ultra-focused* to everything going on around them. Are they "attention deficit?" If they were more "attention deficit" to all those things going on around them, it would actually help them focus. Kids with ADHD are way too attentive, not "attention deficit."

Being open to a flood of thoughts isn't always a bad thing. Goleman's best-selling 2013 book, *FOCUS: The Hidden Driver of Excellence*, identifies something called "open wondering" as a characteristic of the ADHD child's brain. They seem to be better able to let go of the restrictions in the way we are supposed to think and enter into the world of creative thoughts. They have fewer barriers of where their thoughts take them. From this an ADHD child can be very creative and think of amazing ideas outside of the box. Maybe this is why Einstein, who likely had ADHD, was such an incredible and creative inventor. Einstein said intelligence is not about information it's about imagination.

ADHD kids have different brain activity. There is a biological source of ADHD that originates in the front part of the brain (pre-frontal cortex), which is in charge of regulating, organizing and controlling what we choose to focus on, how we choose to behave, and even plays a part in how we respond emotionally. This part of an ADHD child's brain has less neurotransmitter activity (norepinephrine and dopamine) than in children without ADHD.

ADHD kids often do much better when interested or stimulated. Parents and teachers often get confused in that just because their child can focus so well on a specific activity, they must not have ADHD. A parent may say, "My child can focus and play video games for hours with no issues," or, "My child is so organized and responsible with his Pokemon cards." It's a good point, because when the child is engaged in an activity that is interesting and/or stimulating, they usually don't show any signs of ADHD. Even a hyperactive ADHD child may sit perfectly still during a movie they enjoy. But that same child might rotate in an upside-down position in their chair when you try to do math flashcards to help them study for a test.

A good gauge of whether or not a child has ADHD is to ask, "How do they do when the activity is boring or not as stimulating?" We all have problems with boring tasks, but people without ADHD can say to themselves, "This is boring, but I'll push through it and get it done," and end up completing the task. They can make themselves do it. In contrast, an ADHD child may have the same thoughts and good intentions of getting it done, but have serious problems *making* or *willing* themselves to finish the task

ADHD kids will start thinking about something more interesting or what they would rather be doing when uninterested. This becomes a distraction and they end up forgetting or missing an important part of the current task they are doing, resulting in work that is incomplete or work that looks carelessly completed. Here are a few examples:

At home:

- They throw all their clothing in the drawer, but don't fold their clothes first.
- They often forget to flush the toilet or put the lid down.
- They take out the trash, but don't put a new trash bag in the trash can.
- They do the dishes, but don't wipe the counters or start the dishwasher.

At school:

- They turn in their assignment, but don't put their name on it.
- They bring their backpack home, but forget their assignment.
- They finish their homework, but forget to turn it in.

Most missed steps are accidental, but they also may skip a task on purpose to get the job done faster. For example, a child asked to clean up a small milk spill on the floor may decide to quickly use his sock on his foot to soak it up. The task was completed without adding the 4 additional boring steps of (1) walking over to get a paper towel, (2) bringing it back to the spill, (3) bending down to clean it up, and (4) going back to the trash to throw the towel away. Using the sock saved time and allowed him to more quickly move on to what he would rather be doing.

ADHD kids have higher occurrences of learning difficulties. ADHD has nothing to do with how smart a person is, but it can affect their ability to learn new things. These learning challenges can be related to not being able to focus on what is being taught, or they can come from issues with processing information slowly, or issues with short-term memory. Kids with ADHD may also have associated learning disorders like dyslexia or dysgraphia. If your child has ADHD, it is always important to rule out learning disabilities.

ADHD kids have problems filtering or regulating themselves socially, emotionally, and physically. Think of the front part of the brain as a coffee filter (remember, this front part of the brain is where the ADHD physically resides). The job of a coffee filter is to regulate or control what goes into the coffee pot. The filter allows water to go through but not the grounds. The "filter" of an ADHD child isn't working as well as it should. Using this example with ADHD, a child who doesn't have a properly working "filter" in his mind will have more problems regulating what "comes out" through their behavior and emotions.

Let's look at a situation where an ADHD boy is being teased. Multiple ideas pop into his mind about how to react and handle this situation, and because the filter is not working like it should, an inappropriate response may come out, such as pushing or hitting another child. The ADHD child often gets frustrated by his impulsive actions and will make comments that show their self-frustration like, "I can't help it…I don't know why I did that…It just happened so fast."

It's not just emotion or behavior that is affected, but kids with ADHD are often hyperactive. (As mentioned before, girls with ADHD tend to not be as hyperactive as boys with ADHD.) Because they are not filtering their emotions or behavior as well, they may annoy or bother others. A child with an active filter will say to themselves, "I need to sit still now," or "I need to let the other person talk now." But an ADHD child has problems controlling their hyperactivity and impulses. In a classroom setting, instead of waiting their turn, they may just blurt out the answer without waiting to be called on. If they are told to sit still in a chair, they will fidget, tip, bounce, twist, and squirm. Interestingly, physical activity is more regulated when they are doing something they enjoy, like watching TV or playing video games.

When the filter isn't working as well, the teacher or parent often has to act as the filter for that child to help regulate them. The adults have to make comments like, "Stop doing that and start your work," or "I can't understand you, slow down," or "Stop swinging from the curtains." This constant need to help regulate will cause frustration for those working with the child and the ADHD child themselves.

ADHD kids also tend to be hyper-talkers. They may have problems regulating how much and how fast they talk with seemingly no regard for interrupting others. And because their internal thoughts often travel faster than they can talk, what they say may only be part of their point, causing confused communication.

ADHD kids can develop opposition and defiance toward authority, sometimes diagnosed as Oppositional Defiance Disorder. The ADHD child may start defying or arguing with his parents or teachers on a regular basis. This can happen with ADHD children because they are continually frustrated with an adult's frequent prompting and being told what to do or what not to do. Throughout their life they have heard, "Don't put your milk cup so close to the edge of the table," or "You forgot this." They rebel, insisting to do things their own way in order to preserve their dignity.

This defiance can also happen with their friends or peers. Even in play or fun situations, they may want to do things *their* way too often and argue when it doesn't go their way. This can create conflicts in friendships or end friendships all together.

ADHD kids dislike and get frustrated when told to shift from a stimulating activity to a less stimulating activity. Tell an ADHD child who loves watching TV to stop their homework, go turn on the TV, turn the channel to their favorite show, and watch it for an hour, and they will probably do every step you requested without a fight. That's the result of high interest. Tell an ADHD child to turn off their favorite show, start their homework (that they don't like) and turn it in to their teacher tomorrow, and there is usually great resistance. Sure, almost every kid has this problem to a degree. But, shifting from fun to "not as fun" is a *major* problem for ADHD kids and one of the most challenging interactions for parents and teachers.

The mental and physical pace is usually much faster with an ADHD child. Because of that, they can find it challenging to shift from a fast pace to a slower pace. Here are some examples:

- Slowing down to go to bed
- Stopping to take a break or a rest
- Forgetting to eat or drink enough fluids, because they are having so much fun
- Forgetting to use the bathroom when they have a chance (5 minutes into the car ride: "I need to go to the bathroom.")
- Transitioning from recess time to class time

ADHD kids are unable to be bored and are often disruptive or annoy others because of it. ADHD children are experts at turning boring times into more interesting times. The brain of an ADHD child thrives on stimulation and desperately needs to be active. An ADHD child may take "boring spelling" and turn it into "more fun spelling" by talking or joking with friends, tipping in their chair, making sounds with their mouth and drum taps with their hands, or drawing instead of working. Even arguing with the parent or teacher can be a way to avoid doing something they see as boring, as arguing itself can be stimulating (although a negative stimulation).

Have you ever wondered why your ADHD child or student seems to create a little chaos or disruption exactly at the time they are supposed to be quiet? Children with ADHD find ways to be entertained when bored, which often gets them in trouble. In these disruptive times, ask yourself, "Are they bored and is what they are doing adding some spice and excitement to the situation?" Usually they are not aware of how disruptive they are to others in class or at home. Interestingly, they can become frustrated when others are making noises or causing disturbances, even when they were doing the same thing.

ADHD kids may also take higher risks that are dangerous. If they become bored with even a fun activity, they will try to create more excitement. They may climb too high on playground equipment, or as teenagers drive too fast in their car. The risk adds stimulation and excitement which is something ADHD kids thrive on.

ADHD kids get sidetracked. Sometimes in their effort to evade an assignment they are willing to trade a really boring task for a less boring task. An ADHD child may suddenly decide cleaning the cat's litter box or wiping down the kitchen counters is better than starting the long science project they have been putting off.

ADHD kids have problems visualizing how long a task will take. They may think the project will take 1 hour, when in fact it takes 6 hours. They have problems visualizing all of the steps required in that task and therefore are very poor at estimating the time it will take to do all those steps in that task. They become frustrated or sidetracked, and many times that can lead to uncompleted projects.

ADHD kids see a task as one big chunk of work and have difficulty seeing the multiple steps it takes to get that work done. It requires a lot of skill to visualize all the small steps that exist in one task. We often don't think about it. Take the multiple steps in preparing a meal as an example. There is the planning to be sure we have the ingredients first, and making a list of what items are needed. That list should be made with careful strategy according to where items are located in the store, as to avoid back tracking and wasting time. Then when it's time to cook the meal there is a careful and thoughtful process of timing each of the meal items so they are all ready to be served at the same time and at a specific time (the rice broccoli, chicken, etc.), as well as having the table set and serving bowls or platters ready. When you can easily visualize the multiple steps in a task, you tend to be more relaxed in the process of getting that task done. You are also more successful at completing the task on time.

People with ADHD have a hard time seeing multiple steps in a task and tend to see them as just one big chunk of work, which result in them feeling overwhelmed. They may need help breaking down the steps, or at least be reminded, "Hey, this isn't done all at once… it's one step at a time." Typically, kids with ADHD do better with single item concrete assignments rather than multi-item abstract tasks. They typically do better when those tasks and responsibilities are written down or presented to them one at a time, with doable time periods for completion. If told to clean their room, they may miss things you assumed they would do. Remember, "cleaning your room" is a process with many steps. Your child will most likely do better with a check list separating the items out, like "make your bed, put your toys in the box, and dust the top of the dresser," instead of "clean your room."

ADHD kids think boring tasks will "take forever." Some things you request (like taking out the trash) seem so simple and you may wonder why your child is making such a big deal of something that takes less than a minute. For ADHD kids, boring tasks seem to "last forever," or at least take too long, which keeps them away from the interesting things they would rather be doing.

ADHD kids are often disorganized and don't plan ahead. They may start a task or activity, but don't plan ahead in that activity. Here are some examples:

- They went in the bathroom to take a shower but didn't bring a towel.
- They leave for school but didn't grab their jacket even though it's freezing out.
- They finish their homework but didn't put it in their back pack so it can be turned in tomorrow.
- They stay up too late and have to pay the price of being tired the next day.

ADHD kids are focused in the moment; they don't think about what they may need to do later. Adults can relate when they put their car keys in random places, not thinking ahead that finding their keys will be impossible. Kids with ADHD may just throw their homework in an already trashed backpack (the backpack abyss), never to see it again. This lack of planning can cause them to miss assignments and time deadlines.

Planning for boring things just isn't fun. They enjoy "doing something," not "planning to do something." Let's say there is an assignment to create an outline for a paper, then write the paper when they are done with the outline. Instead, the ADHD child may write the paper first to just "get it done," and make the outline later, only because it's a requirement for the grade. Planning takes time and they would rather just go for it. This is why convincing an ADHD child to use a planner is usually met with a ton of resistance.

It's worth noting that there are times when an ADHD child loves planning and can get excited about the planning process. The only time this usually happens is when they are planning for something fun, like getting ready for a birthday party or a camping trip.

ADHD kids hate doing things twice, especially when they disliked it the first time. Imagine watching a two hour movie that you didn't like (you have one in mind I'm sure). When the credits came up you were excited it was over and a little angry it wasted your time and money. Now, imagine that you are required to watch that same movie again the next day or you'll be grounded. Oh, the agony of sitting through it again! This is how it feels to be an ADHD child and having to do something like chores or an assignment again. Even having to make revisions to papers or corrections on tests can be a huge challenge. The first time was enough, but doing it again? NEVER!

ADHD kids jump ahead. You may see your ADHD child jump ahead in conversations or directions because their inside thoughts travel faster than others. They don't want to wait. They think they already know what you are going to say and finish your sentence for you. Or they say "I know, I know, I know," before you are done. If you don't get to the point, they may get to the point for you. They might start their school project without hearing the details or complete directions. They listen to part of what a person is saying, then assume the rest. However, they are much more patient when *they* are talking.

Waiting their turn with peers can also be challenging. They may impulsively demand to go first or argue to go first, because waiting is difficult. This can frustrate their friends and peers.

ADHD kids have problems with delayed gratification. They are much more motivated for short term more frequent rewards (that are smaller) than they are for rewards that require a long waiting period (even if it's a larger reward). That is why rewarding a child for good grades at the end of the quarter often is not effective because it is too long term. Rewarding a child daily or weekly for the process of doing their schoolwork, rather than for the grade itself, will have a much better impact and will ultimately result in better grades.

ADHD kids put things off and procrastinate. An analogy regarding ADHD is to imagine a boy sitting on a railroad track. We say to him, "Hey, you should get off the track because we know a train is coming soon." The child continues to sit there, even as he sees the train coming. Only as the train approaches to about 10 feet away does he finally stand up and get off the track; all the while, we as parents and teachers are anxious and freaking out watching the whole thing. Why didn't he just get off the track when we told him? We knew the train would eventually be there. In this analogy, the boy only acted when he knew he had no other choice but to move. Until then, he could do other more interesting things. He waited until the last minute and only then, when he knew he couldn't wait any longer, was he finally motivated to get up. We talked about how kids with ADHD are more engaged when stimulated. Waiting until the last minute is stimulating; although obviously not always healthy due to the consequences of anxiety and stress.

ADHD kids are notorious for saying, "I'll do it later," only to have it never get done. Often they really do have good intentions to get the task finished later, but if it's out of sight, it's out of mind. Even if they have started the uninteresting task and will "finish it later," they still usually don't complete it fully. Because they forget, they need to be prompted over and over again by their parent or teacher. This frustrates both the child and the adult.

Conclusion

WHEN A PARENT learns their child has ADHD, there can be a mix of emotions. Some parents feel relieved, because the diagnosis tells them why their child is struggling. But knowing your child has ADHD and knowing what can be done about it are two different things. The first part of this book was written to help parents understand the true nature of what childhood ADHD is all about. Section Two will focus on strategies a parent can use to help their ADHD child find success—at home, at school, and in the future.

My Child Has ADHD— Now What?

The Power of Acceptance

THERE ARE MANY strategies parents can use to help their ADHD child. But before discussing those strategies, it's important to be aware that some people will be unaccepting or uneducated about ADHD. You may hear comments like:

- "It's just an excuse not to do their school work."
- "They could do it if they put their mind to it."
- "They are capable of getting better grades if they tried."
- "They are just lazy."
- "Kids will be kids. This is normal. They can control themselves when they want."
- "All kids are hyperactive."

These types of statements assert that children with ADHD are in complete control of what they are doing and minimize the suffering ADHD children experience.

Some parents or teachers will resist or even refuse to give special help to an ADHD child because they feel the help is "enabling" the child. Enabling, when used in this negative way, refers to behavior that is not confronting another person's dysfunction, but is only helping the dysfunction to continue. They may say the child with ADHD "needs to learn to advocate for themselves and learn to do things on their own." That's a true statement. However, there is a balance between giving too much help (which, in fact, *could* be enabling) and not offering enough help. Too much help could make a child overly dependent on others, which could be considered enabling the child. But not offering enough help or offering no help at all can lead to the ADHD child feeling defeated and failing. A parent needs to be open to the idea that there are certainly times when too much help results in the child becoming overly dependent. When that happens, encourage your child not to rely on services or help they don't need in order to become more independent.

A parent will often have to defend the position that accepting and assisting somebody with a disability is not enabling or making excuses. Accepting your child's current state of disability and intervening to improve the current state of ability is not "enabling" or "giving excuses." It is called empowering.

The school staff must show acceptance and knowledge of ADHD. Otherwise, the child will suffer emotionally. The majority of school staff members are supportive of ADHD children, but too often, from the student's point of view, it seems the opposite. When an ADHD student is asked, "Tell me what your teachers think of you," sadly they say things like, "They don't like me," "They think I'm annoying," "They think I'm a bad student," or worse, and not uncommon is, "They hate me." The student may feel that way even if the teacher is doing all they can to support the child.

This perspective is not just limited to school. Children with ADHD often feel they are letting their parents down. When they are pushed too far beyond their limits and abilities, or worse, blamed for their lack of effort, they experience a high degree of stress and self-defeat. A parent saying, "This keeps happening. Why can't you do this?" makes the child think, "Something is wrong with me. What's my problem?" This feeling, in turn, increases anxiety and depression in ADHD children. If ADHD is left untreated, research shows that at least 25% of ADHD children will develop a diagnosis of anxiety, depression, and/or oppositional defiant disorder. (http://www.mentalhelp.net/poc/view_doc.php?type=doc&id=13851&cn=3)

We need to empower a child with ADHD to realize that even though they may struggle, they are capable and can find ways to be successful. This requires adults to be sensitive, understanding and accepting that they are dealing with something real—ADHD. By educating yourself about ADHD, you will be better prepared to help a child with ADHD.

Therefore, the first and most important step to helping a child with ADHD is understanding and acceptance. Even with good intentions, we can all fall into a "non-acceptance" thinking pattern without realizing it. When a child has a physical disability, such as a cast on their leg, it's easier to see and accept the person's limitations. They certainly wouldn't be told to run a mile in gym class. But when the disability is internal, such as ADHD, it's understandably more challenging to remember there are legitimate limitations.

A parent or teacher may get frustrated about their ADHD child continuing to get off task while doing their schoolwork. What *should* be 30 minutes of work is taking more like 60 minutes. They are messing around half the time. It's easy to think, "They *should* be able to control themselves and stay on task like the other kids." But can an ADHD child sit still and stay on task for a full 30 minutes? Do they have the capacity to do this? This is where education and acceptance are important.

Too often, "should" statements, either said in your mind or out loud, can be a sign that you don't fully accept your child's ADHD symptoms. Non-acceptance leads to frustration for both you and your child. But, you can instantly lower frustration by having a realistic expectation and acceptance of who your child is. This doesn't mean you always need to agree with your child's behavior, it just means you accept "why it's happening" and work from there.

Think of it this way. Imagine if, every morning, you woke up expecting your coffee maker to make lemonade. Each time it made coffee instead, and you would be upset it didn't make the lemonade you expected. But why? If you simply accepted that a coffee maker makes coffee (and not lemonade) you wouldn't be frustrated and your mind would be more at ease. That's acceptance.

With acceptance, a parent will understand that their ADHD child has great difficulty staying on task with long assignments. With acceptance, the parent would *expect* there's a good chance that a long assignment is going to be a challenge and will be prepared. That parent may say, "Let's work for 20-30 minutes and then take a 10-minute break. You can finish the rest after that."

What about school? Why would we *expect* a hyperactive ADHD child to sit perfectly still during a one-hour class when previous history has shown they can't do that? By accepting who the child is, the teacher might find more success by giving more frequent breaks or by allowing the student to have something to fidget with in their hand.

One last example: What if your child forgets to bring home their homework packet for the twelfth time? Instead of lecturing, "Why did you forget your homework again? You have to do better," a more productive response would be, "I know remembering your schoolwork is one of your challenges. Let's talk about a better plan to remember next time." Comments of "how could you" or "you should know by now" only make things worse.

Part of acceptance is knowing that you, as the parent, will have to act as a manager and give regular prompts and reminders to your child. This takes a lot of extra work and isn't fun for either of you. Until they can demonstrate reliable self-management, you may have to keep track of things like homework, chores and scheduled activities. All of your interventions are aimed toward the idea that your child will eventually do these tasks independently.

Be your child's biggest supporter, advocate, and believer. Count on no one else taking this critical position, as you will be their main, and sometimes only, advocate. Children with ADHD routinely question their own abilities and they need to know you believe in them and are there to help. Let them know you understand their struggles, and even when it gets tough, you're not giving up. You are their cheerleader!

Don't get caught arguing in your mind, "Why does it have to be this way?" It's okay to feel sorry for yourself for a few minutes, but feeling sorry for yourself longer than that doesn't get you anywhere. It's much more productive to say to yourself, "it is what it is" and work with the reality of what you have in front of you. Country artist Kacey Musgraves said it best in one of her songs where she sings, "It is what it is, 'til it ain't anymore." Accept what is and work towards positive change.

Conclusion:

When you practice acceptance, you will find the interactions with your child to be more understanding and compassionate. Acceptance is the starting point in helping your ADHD child. Without it, a child is more prone to feelings of inadequacy, leading to increased stress and/or depression. With acceptance, your child is more likely to feel supported, understood and cared for. They will feel better about who they are and what they can do. There will be less frustration and more motivation to face challenges head on.

Understanding Your Child's Behavior

WHEN WORKING TO change your child's behavior, you first need to understand why the behavior happened. If this isn't understood, strategies to change your child's behavior will not be effective. This chapter provides insight regarding why your child behaves the way they do and offers solutions for how to change undesirable behaviors.

Temperament Matches and Differences

A child's behavior is greatly influenced by their temperament. Our temperament is the predisposition of the person we are at birth and has nothing to do with the influence of parenting or how we are raised. Comments from parents like, "Since she was born, she has always been so easy going," is really a comment on the child's temperament. Here is a list of nine temperament traits that people have in varying degrees and intensity:

1. Activity Level: Your child's degree or amount of physical or verbal activity.

2. Regularity: Your child's tendency to be routine or degree of sameness—eating, sleeping, etc.—are regular (predictable) or irregular (unpredictable).

3. Adaptability: Your child's ability to shift or adjust to their environment.

4. Approach/Withdrawal: Your child's comfort level in engaging with people or situations.

5. Physical Sensitivity: Your child's sensitivity regarding taste, sight, hearing, smell, touch.

6. Intensity of Reaction: Your child's typical level of emotional reactions.

7. Distractibility: Your child's overall ability to stay focused and on task.

8. Positive or Negative Mood: Your child's general mood and outlook on life.

9. Persistence: Your child's overall level of sticking to things and not giving up.[1]

When a parent and child have differences in temperament traits, conflicts between them are more likely to happen. In order to master more effective parenting, it's important to recognize where there are temperament trait differences between you and your child.

EXAMPLE: A parent and their child have differences with "adaptability." (trait #3) The parent is easily able to stop one activity and transition to another, while the child tends to have problems stopping what they are doing and needs 5-10 minutes to move to another task. This parent says to their child who is playing outside, "It's time to come inside for dinner," and expects their child to stop immediately and come inside. However, the child takes 5 minutes to finally come inside. Because the parent has no problems with transitioning from one activity to another, they may feel frustrated and think, "Why can't she just come in when I tell her to? It's not that difficult." The child thinks, "I can't just drop everything I'm

---

1 Thomas A. and S. Chess, Temperament and Development (New York: Brunner-Mazel, 1977)

doing. I was right in the middle of something." Their difference in "adaptability" is bound to cause tension and conflict.

SOLUTION: The parent must be aware of their temperament differences and make adjustments. Being aware that their child has problems with adaptability, the parent could make a simple adjustment and give their child a "10-minute warning" when they need to come in for dinner. This approach would allow for more transition time and will likely lessen the frustration experienced for both the parent and the child.

A parent can make adjustments, but in the real world, people aren't going to adjust to your child's temperament traits. For example, when your child is an adult, their boss probably won't say, "Hey, this is the fifth time you are late to work… *but* because I know you have problems transitioning, I'll let this go and call to remind you next time." As the child gets older, it's a parent's job to help their child be aware of *who they are* (their temperament) and teach their child how to adapt who they are to the "real world." In truth, that task is the basic principle of what parenting is all about. Here are some steps to get this started:

1. Identify the level of intensity of each trait for both the parent and child. You can use a 1-10 scale where "10" represents the most and "1" represents the least.

2. Accept your child's temperament, even if it seems unreasonable (such as your child seeming overly emotional).

3. Examine the trait differences between the parent and child and think about where and when these differences may cause problems.

4. Adjust your parenting strategies to better accommodate your child's temperament.

5. As your child gets older, help them to understand their temperament traits and how to make adjustments for the "real world."

The Unacceptable Behavior Works

A child behaves the way they do because the behavior simply *works* for your child in some way. The behavior may be seen as undesirable to the parent, but is the behavior undesirable to the child?

EXAMPLE: Let's say your child has been lying to you by saying, "I don't have any homework." Although lying is not appropriate behavior, lying "worked" for them because they had more free time to play video games that week.

SOLUTION: You will need to figure out why the undesired behavior is working for them and find a way to make it not "work" anymore. In this lying example above, the child was able to play video games because the parent took the child's word that they didn't have homework. To fix this problem, the parent could be in direct contact and get homework information from the teacher until their child proves they are reliable about telling the truth. If they lie about homework, consequences will be given. Saying, "I don't have any homework," will not "work" anymore and so lying about not having homework will likely stop.

Our Thoughts and Emotions

A child's behavior is greatly influenced by their thoughts and emotions. Here is the sequence of how behaviors happen:

1) Something happens around us in our environment.
2) The mind interprets what just happened and we put a thought or opinion to it.
3) An emotion develops based on that thought or opinion.
4) When influenced by both that thought and emotion, a behavior happens.

EXAMPLE: In class, the teacher assigns a project due next week. The child has an initial thought of, "I can't get that done in time... I'll fail that assignment." The child may not even be fully aware that they had that thought. They start feeling anxio s, sad and angry. Because of those thoughts and emotions, the child ends up avoiding the project and decides not to do it because "they can't and they will fail anyway".

SOLUTION: When an undesirable behavior develops, it's a very important first step to help your child be aware of their initial thoughts and help them challenge those thoughts for accuracy. In the previous example, the thought would be "I can't get that done in time... I'll fail that assignment." Help them be aware that they had that thought and ask them, "Is it *really true* you *can't* get this done in time?" and "Is it *really true* you are going to *fail*?" You may need to remind them, "Remember that other difficult assignment you had last month?... You finished that on time and got a 75%, not a failing grade." When they realize their thoughts were not completely accurate and they believe the truth that they actually can do the project, there can be an immediate impact on improving emotions and behavior. Now more optimistic, they will likely be more hopeful and motivated to start and finish their project.

Often, children feel misunderstood. It's important to validate the thoughts and emotions of your child, even if *you* think those thoughts and emotions aren't warranted or justified. Validating doesn't mean you have to agree, but that you can understand their viewpoint. A child is much more open to talking if they feel heard and understood. This is especially true if you are trying to change undesirable behaviors. If feelings aren't accepted or validated, a child is more likely to engage in the same undesirable behaviors again. If there is a significant emotional outburst, that's a BIG SIGN to the parent to stop, slow down, look your child in the eyes, and calmly hear them out. Here is an example of accepting and validating emotions:

"I understand how you think there is no time to get your project done. That's stressful. I can see how that would make you want to avoid starting your work."

Once the child feels heard, they are usually much less defensive and much more willing to open up to you. Understanding is always the starting point.

Your Child Is Copying Another Person's Behavior

Children copy behaviors, both desirable and otherwise, from their parents, other adults, siblings, friends, television shows, etc.

EXAMPLE: A parent raises their voice when feeling frustrated with their child. The child learns this behavior and also starts raising their voice when angry at their parent. Or, an older sibling often uses the words, "you're stupid" to others in the family and the younger children start saying, "you're stupid" to others in the family.

SOLUTION: When analyzing why a child behaves the way they do, it's important to look around to see who they could possibly be copying. It may be that you need to focus on changing *that* person's behavior first.

It's important to role model the good behaviors you want from your child. It's extremely challenging to change behaviors that even parents continue to engage in themselves. If you want your child to be better at getting their tasks done, role model that behavior for them. For example, if a parent neglects or forgets obligations or tasks themselves, it sends a confusing message to the child if they are then punished for doing the same thing.

Your Child's Behavior Is Reactive

A child's behavior is greatly influenced by the way others interact with them. Children are very keen, observant and reactive to the way others treat them. This is especially true when they sense disapproval or rejection from others.

EXAMPLE: After a couple of weeks failing spelling tests, the parent yells in frustration, "Come on… you're not trying hard enough!" The parent's response immediately puts the child in a defensive position and makes them anxious about having a future negative interaction with the parent. So in the next spelling test, the child cheats on the test in order to avoid parental disapproval and anger.

SOLUTION: Cheating is obviously not appropriate but, right or wrong, the parent's behavior of anger and displaying a high level of disapproval significantly influenced the decision of this child to cheat. The child became desperate in order to avoid a harsh reaction of disapproval from their parent. Be aware of how your behavior and reactions influence your child's behavior. How do you react when your child does well? How do you react when your child does something wrong? Are your reactions making things better or worse? Are they helping to promote change or not?

Make sure your responses are supportive, kind and respectful. Blaming comments like, "what's your problem" doesn't work for anyone! A better response to them failing their spelling test might be, "Hey, this spelling is frustrating and I know you have been trying… let's try going over the spelling words together the night before the test to see if that helps."

Be careful to limit and/or avoid long lectures. Kids tune those out quickly anyway. First, give your child a chance to express their own feelings and thoughts about the situation without interruption. You may be surprised that they may say what you had planned to say anyway. Repeat back to them what you heard and make sure you got it right, allowing them to clarify. Your child feeling heard is a big deal and should give you an idea of a better solution and a better way to respond.

Your Child Wants to be a Good Kid, Not a Bad One

One of the main desires of a child is to matter to their parent and to be a good kid. Even if a child doesn't say or show it, 99% of the time they want you, as the parent, to show your approval and be proud of them. If children feel their parents aren't proud of them, they often conclude they are a "bad kid" in their parent's eye and start to lose that desire to please them. This is not good! When a child doesn't care anymore what their parent thinks, a child is more prone to have undesirable behaviors.

Children also desire to be a "good student" to their teachers as well. Behavior starts going downhill once they start to think, "I'm not a good student," or "My teacher doesn't like me." The child may start to think, "I don't care what my teacher thinks of me, they don't like me anyway."

EXAMPLE: A child may be failing multiple subjects at school and because of that, may start feeling like a failure. Their poor school performance has really started taking a hit on their self-esteem and feeling of self-worth. Both the teacher and parent continue voicing disapproval for their "lack of effort." Feeling increasingly discouraged that they can "never please their teacher or parent," they may start refusing to do their work in class and at home.

SOLUTION: When trying to understand behavior, it's important to understand that a child's feelings of self-worth are connected to their behavior. The better they feel about themselves, the more favorable their behavior will be and the more motivated they will become. In contrast, the more inadequate they feel about themselves, the more acting out behavior they will have and the less motivated they will become. It's important that they feel support and understanding.

To help foster improved self-worth in your child, focus on the positive behaviors as much as possible. Don't we all feel better about ourselves when the focus is on what we are doing well rather than what we are doing wrong? Aim toward this guideline: 75% of your comments should be positive and 25% corrective in a positive way.

There will be days when it's difficult to find the 75% positives, but you still need to do it. Each day, search for something your child has done well and tell your child you noticed. Say something like, "Good work on that math test," or "Nice job getting that project done on time… that was a lot of work." Also, make sure to tell them every once in a while, "I'm proud of you," and be able to back it up with why. It's important to let them know you value *who they are* as a person inside (such as being funny or caring) much more than *what they do* (like getting an "A" on the test or winning a race).

It's also worth bringing up again the importance of schoolwork expectations matching their capacity and ability. One sure way to foster feelings of failure and inadequacy is having schoolwork expectations that are far beyond what they are capable of actually doing.

When your child doesn't do well with something, make sure to be kind and encouraging. Make sure they know that even when they fail, that doesn't change how you feel about them. Let them know, "I understand you are feeling down about that test. I'd be frustrated too. I'm sure you will do better next time. I still love you and am proud of how hard you are trying."

Children Want to be More and More Independent

From birth to adulthood, children are naturally motivated to become more independent. That's a good thing. It's very common for a child to express anger when a parent does not allow enough independence. This is especially true as they get into their late teen years. Because ADHD children often need significant parental and teacher assistance, they often feel they are not getting enough independence. If this "assistance" is done in the wrong way, they may feel that adults are "in their business" too much. This can cause them to become more resistant.

EXAMPLE: A parent reminds their teenager 5-6 times in one hour that "they'd better get started on their homework." The teen responds in anger, "I know, leave me alone!" The parent has good reason to keep reminding them, because they often put off doing their work until the last minute. The teen starts to feel that getting their homework done is now more for their parent's benefit and not for themselves. The parental reminders make it worse and the teen starts to think about not doing the work at all.

SOLUTION: Walking the fine line between encouraging independence and providing the necessary assistance to your ADHD child is tough. Parents often feel "you're darned if you do and darned if you don't." Parents should always think about ways to allow their child to have some independence. If your child wants to do it their way and "their system" works, let them do it their way. If their system doesn't work, then talk together to come up with another agreeable solution. You can make a mutual decision with your child that you will not prompt them to get started with their homework anymore if they start by themselves at the agreed time. But tell them if it doesn't work their way, it will need to be done your way. In this case, they will be reminded and required to start their homework at 4 p.m. Go back to trying it "their way" after they have been successful in doing their work at 4 p.m. for two days without arguing. There should always be movement toward independence, if they can handle it.

Break in Routine

When things are familiar or routine in our environment, our brain doesn't need to work as hard in analyzing what's going on around us. People are comforted and calmed by sameness and routine. Try wearing your watch on your other wrist, or change the driver seat position in your car and you will quickly realize how much this is true (at least at first). When a person is forced to change the familiar and routine in their life or when the expected becomes unexpected, it triggers discomfort, stress and irritability. Having a change, or break in routine, is a common source of acting out behavior.

EXAMPLE: A 7-year-old child has become accustomed to being picked up from school, going home and watching cartoons right away. On the drive home, Mother announces a change in routine. "When you get home today, you need to finish your chores before watching T.V." At that point the child gets angry and yells, "WHAT? NO, I'M NOT! I'M WATCHING MY SHOW FIRST LIKE I'VE BEEN DOING MY WHOLE ENTIRE LIFE!!!" The parent has to debate and argue with their child for the next hour before the chores are finally done.

SOLUTION: For children, and especially ADHD children, it's all about routine, constancy, predictability and sameness. Do things the same way, at the same time and at the same place. This obviously means that the parent needs to be on top of things to make sure this happens. It's not going to work if the parent is out of routine, inconsistent or unpredictable with their expectations. Sure, there are many times where things happen that can't be controlled or aren't part of our routine. For things that come up like that, it's best to give your child as much advance notice as possible to allow them to prepare or process the change in routine. In the example above, if the parent wanted to change the routine to require doing chores before T.V. time, it would have worked much better to give a day or more notice by saying, "Starting Monday, before you start watching T.V. we are making a new rule that chores need to be done first." There may still be resistance, but it's going to go much better than giving a last minute notice.

It's Not Fair

One remark that is universal with children across the globe and in different languages is the comment "NO FAIR!" Children are preoccupied with fairness and being treated equally. Really, the same can be said for adults. The only difference is that adults say "no fair" in their minds and don't yell it out loud (well most don't).

When kids perceive that others are treated better, it makes them feel they are valued less or that they're not as important. This is a significant trigger of sadness and anger for both children and adults. If perceived unfairness continues for months or years, self-comments such as, "I'm not worth being treated better," or "I deserve to be treated worse," can set in. This is not good. Bitterness or increased depression can set in and become a serious problem. Sometimes these feelings can turn into aggressive behavior toward those who are perceived as being "treated better."

EXAMPLE: A child yells "THAT'S NO FAIR" after finding out her little sister only needs to vacuum while she has the bigger task of cleaning the entire bathroom. The father states, "It's fair because you are older and your little sister isn't able to do what you can." After more arguing, the father states simply, "Life's not fair—get used to it." Regardless of the rationale, it still frustrates her and she continues to be bitter toward her father for the rest of the morning. She starts to perceive a regular pattern of her little sister being treated better "all the time" and one day pushes her sister to the ground in frustration.

SOLUTION: The first part of the solution is to be understanding and validate the need we all have for fairness. Of course, not everything is fair in this world and children need to accept this and learn to adapt. But in order to accept this, it's helpful for the parent to take time to explain the situation and reasoning behind "why it's fair." The simple "life isn't fair" statement doesn't help.

It's human nature to want to be treated fairly and there is nothing wrong with a parent or teacher doing what they can to help foster fairness at home and at school. Don't minimize your child's need for fairness. It's not just a "child thing." If an employee at work does one job and finds out they get paid half the amount of another employee who did the exact same job yesterday, they may yell "NO FAIR" also.

With the chores example, offering the older sibling extra chore money for the more difficult chore is perfectly acceptable. If concerns are brought up that the situation isn't fair, it's okay to say "good point" and change things up. Fostering fairness helps foster a peaceful environment.

It's a Misunderstanding

Someone misunderstanding the true intention of another person's behavior is a major reason for misbehavior or conflict in relationships. This isn't just true in parent– child relationships, but other relationships too—friends, spouses, and co-workers. Misunderstandings are a normal part of life and happen frequently throughout the day.

EXAMPLE: As a parent helps their child assemble the science fair project, the parent notices their child is getting increasingly frustrated. The parent assumes it's because their child doesn't want them helping, so the parent calmly says, "I'm going to let you work on it more by yourself, but call me over if you need more of my help." The child is confused and thinks their parent is upset at how long it's taking to finish the project. In reality, the parent was not upset, but was trying to be helpful by leaving. And the child was not angry at the parent at all, but was frustrated that the glue wasn't sticking to the poster board like it should. They misunderstood the intent of the other person's behavior.

SOLUTION: In relationships, the only way to clear up possible misunderstandings is to calmly communicate with each other. The parent could have asked, "Are you getting frustrated with me helping you?" and the child would have clarified, "No, I'm actually angry about the glue not working." Conflict is often reduced or resolved once the true intention of a behavior is communicated.

Behaviors Out of Their Control

It's important to note that there are certain behaviors that really are not within a child's complete control. When trying to understand a behavior, three questions should be asked:

1. Was this on purpose?
2. Was this out of their control?
3. Was this a little of both (some control)?

Be aware of things that are not within your child's control. If a child is blamed for things that they can't control or have limited control of, this is a set-up for creating anger, anxiety and/or depression. The ADHD symptoms of impulsivity and hyperactivity are examples of behaviors not "done on purpose." There is obviously a very long list of things that can influence behaviors, where a child is in limited control or no control at all. The following list is just a small sample of things that can influence behavior where a child is likely to have limited or no control:

- Tourette's or Tic Disorder (sounds or movements)
- Bi-Polar Disorder (irritability, rages, obsessiveness, irrational thinking, grandiosity, risk taking, or mentally ramped up)
- Depression and/or grief and loss (irritability, sadness, crying, hopelessness, low energy, lacking motivation, problems paying attention, not caring)
- Lack of sleep or being hungry (irritable / grumpiness, moodiness, lack of concentration, low energy, low frustration tolerance)
- Body pains such as back pain or headache (irritability, low frustration tolerance, problems concentrating, lack of work motivation, moodiness, depression)
- Obsessive Compulsive Disorder (irritability, anxiety, problems concentrating, problems transitioning, problems getting out of obsessive thought process and letting go)

- Post-Traumatic Stress Disorder or Anxiety Disorders (irritability, problems concentrating, anxiety, fear, over-reactions, anger, avoidance, over thinking)

- Various medical conditions such as Diabetes or Crohn's Disease OR neurological disorders such as Multiple Sclerosis (low energy, problems concentrating, low motivation, irritability, confusion, anger, discouragement, hopelessness, moodiness, stress, depression)

It's important to be aware that there are some cases of behavior where a child is not in complete control. In those cases, the parent needs to assess, "How much of this is within their control or is being done on purpose?" Adjust your own response depending on the answer to that question.

Conclusion

If a parent desires to change some of their child's behaviors, they must first work to understand why the behavior is happening in the first place. Once this is done, a parent can then take steps toward changing the undesirable behaviors to more favorable behaviors.

At the end of this book (pages 122-125), I've provided two worksheets to help you better understand behaviors. One is titled "Understanding the Behaviors and Intention of Others" and the other is called "Did Your Behavior Work?" Both worksheets are designed to help you and your child better understand a specific behavior, the intention of that behavior, and the outcome of that behavior.

Motivating Behavior Change

CHANGING THE UNDESIRABLE behaviors of a child can be very challenging, especially when they don't desire or care to change these behaviors. The old saying, "You can lead a horse to water, but you can't make it drink," definitely applies to ADHD kids. To change your child's behaviors, you need to find leverage. This chapter gives strategies to help promote the behaviors you want from your child and put a stop to the behaviors you don't.

Using a Privilege Reward System

One way to help motivate behavioral change is a privilege reward system. Privileges are things that need to be earned such as going to a friend's house, playing video games, or having a cell phone. Make sure your child knows what items or activities are considered a privilege and which are not. If they are behaving appropriately, they are allowed their privileges. If not, they simply lose their privileges until they do what is expected. If the privilege needs to be denied, stay positive and calmly tell them, "Tomorrow you have another chance," or "Only when you finish your chore list can you watch T.V." Let them know they had a choice in the matter. You don't want them thinking it's your fault and they were a victim. When a privilege is not earned, there may be some backlash and anger from the child. Don't give in!

If behaviors aren't improving after 4-6 days, modify your expectations. For example, a parent may need to reduce required reading time from 45 minutes to 30 minutes, due to their child being overly busy with other important obligations that day. Your child being successful is an important part of this system working.

Using a Token Reward System.

Similar to a privilege reward system, a token reward system focuses on allowing your child to earn tokens when a desired behavior happens. The "token" can be poker chips, tickets, or marbles (although poker chips seem to be the easiest to use and don't get lost as easily). Have your child store these tokens in a special place to make sure they don't lose them. Once a pre-determined token amount is earned, your child can then trade the tokens in for a reward.

When first starting the token reward system, try to set things up so that your child is able to earn enough tokens to trade in for a reward during the first week, if not more. Being successful in the first week allows them to "buy into the system."

Kids prefer rewards that don't take as long to earn. Make sure tokens can be earned at least daily. For kids with more challenging behavior, it's sometimes necessary to make sure tokens can be earned at least hourly. That's especially true for younger children. Offer smaller items or privileges they can spend their tokens on each day. For example, they can earn one Pokémon card for only two tokens. If they have a good day, they can earn that prize 2-3 times in one day. Getting a daily reward is extremely motivating and therefore effective in modifying behavior. If your child wants to aim for bigger rewards, like a new skate board, let them go for it. It may take a lot longer, but this teaches the important life skill of delayed gratification.

It's best to focus on no more than 1-3 behaviors at a time. Make sure the reward or prize they can earn with their tokens is exciting enough to motivate your child.

Just like with the privilege reward system, make sure you are not expecting perfection. You need to start where your child is and make progress from there. For example, you may want to say to yourself "good enough," even if your child says, "Going to bed is so stupid," as long as they went to bed right away without the yelling. Sure, it would have been nice to see them gracefully say, "Yes, momma... have pleasant dreams. Good night." But the fact that they went to bed without yelling is a starting point. Give them a token and let them experience some success. Eventually you can make it more challenging by letting them know that they can't say anything negative back in order to earn the token.

If you have a teenager, using tokens will likely not work. They are going to be just a little bit annoyed if you come to them with the idea of rewarding them with tokens (but who knows...maybe they would like it). With teens, instead of tokens, you could use check marks on the calendar or a clipboard. They can then earn a reward for getting a predetermined number of check marks. You may decide that if they get four days of getting their work done without being told, they can earn a video game rental for the weekend.

It's better to focus on rewarding the process rather than the outcome. For example, instead of having one large reward for good grades at the end of the semester, it's much more effective to give smaller rewards every week your child gets all their homework turned in on time. Rewarding for the work being turned in will likely result in the desired outcome of good grades at the end of the semester anyway. Rewarding just for good grades at the end of the semester usually fails because it isn't focusing enough on the actual problem (such as not turning in homework) and it is too far out to actually motivate their behavior.

When tokens are earned, avoid taking them away for misbehavior. When your child earns a token, it represents something they did that was "good." If you start taking them away, kids may start to dislike the token system and associate the tokens with something negative or something that will be used against them later.

Desperate times call for desperate measures. When rewards don't seem to be working, it's time to add some spark. Adding a bigger and more exciting reward may be temporarily needed to keep things moving forward. For example, the parent may buy a new video game that can be earned by the end of the week. Don't use this "bigger reward" tactic too often; otherwise it loses its leverage because they start to expect the bigger reward every time.

Praising

When trying to change undesirable behavior, it's crucial that the parent recognize the child's positive behaviors as much as possible. It's understandably easy to forget to say anything when your child is behaving well, and give them more attention when they are not behaving well. When your child is doing well, make sure they know that you noticed and tell them why you think what they did was a good thing. For example, a parent could say, "Hey that was really nice that you shared with your sister. I know that made her feel really good and I bet she will want to share more of her things with you now." In this example, the parent not only praised the behavior, but explained more in detail why it was a big deal. Praising is a simple way to motivate your child to behave better. And it's free!

This may sound strange, but for some children who are oppositional and defiant, be careful about praising them for things *you* wanted them to do. Saying, "Good job starting your work when I said," could be interpreted as, "Good job recognizing that I, as the parent, am in charge of you and that you are doing it my way." At times like this, praising can actually work against the parent. However, for an oppositional and defiant child, praising them when it was *their* idea works very well. If you're not sure, you can always ask, "Does saying good job help or make things worse?"

Say What You Want, Not What You Don't

It's more effective to say what you *want* rather than saying what you *don't* want. It's easy to say, "Stop doing that," but this statement doesn't say much. It doesn't instruct the child on what you want done instead. For example, a lifeguard at a pool can yell out to a child, "Don't run!" But yelling out, "Walk!" is more effective because it not only addresses the problem behavior, but it also instructs the child what to do instead. No guess work is needed. Saying clearly what you *want* is more effective than stating what you *don't* want.

Natural Negative Consequences

There are times when a parent needs to allow their child to experience the natural consequence of their own behaviors. As a parent, it's easy to "protect" your child so they don't have to feel hurt, embarrassed or disappointed. However, a child needs to go through some amount of frustration or discomfort in order to learn how the world works. This is how they build resilience. This isn't saying you should always allow your child to "pay the price of their behaviors," but there are times it's beneficial to allow them to face the result of what they chose to do. They will learn from this experience. This is called a natural consequence.

EXAMPLE: A parent works as hard as they can to make sure their 17-year-old son is out the door and in his car on time, so he won't be late for school. This morning routine is always a fight because their child pushes back every day. In the past when their child was late, the parent had called the school to excuse him for being late so he didn't get in trouble. However, is this really helping their child? No, it's not. So, one night, the mother tells their 17-year-old, "I'm no longer going to push you to leave for school on time… and I'm also not going to call the school anymore to excuse your tardiness if you are late." That week their child arrives late to school and the mother discusses the situation with the principal and explains that she isn't going to excuse the lateness. That day, the principal calls the child down to the office and gives him a Saturday detention for being late. In this example, the child had to directly face the consequence of his behavior. Many times this natural consequence can change the behavior around all by itself.

Punishment

Punishment given to a child needs to be for the purpose of helping the child learn and change their behavior; not for the sake of helping the parent feel better or to give the parent a feeling of "justice." Punishment should never involve:

- Shame
- Humiliation
- Embarrassment
- Physical harm
- Emotional harm (such as name calling or put downs)

If punishment is the only strategy being used to change behavior or is being used too often, it becomes ineffective and harmful to the healthy development of a child and to the parent-child relationship. Many parents grew up where punishment was the only thing used "back in their day" and feel "if it worked for me, it will work for my child." Some parents are against giving rewards for "good" behavior. The truth is, as time goes on, we learn more and more about human development and professionals have found that focusing on rewarding the "good" or desirable behaviors is much more beneficial than just focusing on punishing the "bad" behaviors. Focusing on the positive helps build confidence and improves the mental health of a child. Punishment, either used as the only strategy or used too often, breaks down a child's confidence and can damage a child's mental health.

Types of Punishment / Consequences:

■ Grounding or Restrictions

Grounding a child involves immediately restricting or taking away something that is a privilege for a set amount of time. When it's time to take privileges away, make sure that the time restricted from privileges is somehow connected to resolving the problem. Let's say your child is grounded because they have missing work in two of their classes. It's much more productive to say, "Have your teacher write me a note at the end of the week that says all your work was turned in and you can have your privileges back." Or let's say your child didn't do their chores today. It's more productive to say, "If you show me tomorrow that you can get your chores done without arguing, you can have your privileges back." It *doesn't* work as well if you just say, "You're grounded for two weeks," with no requirement for your child to actually work to resolve the problem.

Be careful about restricting privileges too long, as this can actually work against you. If you take all privileges away, you will lose leverage with your child and that's a bad thing. Don't do that to yourself! Make the restriction just long enough that your child gets the point and changes their behavior. If that means they change their behavior after only one day of restrictions, that's great. If it works, it works! Don't ask why.

■ The "3 Strike Rule"

This system is similar to baseball's "3 strikes, you're out" rule. A child is given 3 chances to change their behavior around before they are given a punishment or consequence. For example, if your child is arguing about doing homework or chores, they will get "1 strike." Make sure they know what constitutes "1 strike." If they accumulate "3 strikes" they will lose all privileges that day. For younger children, it can be more effective to restrict privileges for 1 hour, allowing them to "try again" within the hour to earn privileges. It also may be helpful to give a warning that they are about to get a strike. Make sure not to quickly give one strike after another if your child is breaking down or in a crisis. In those situations, they aren't thinking rationally and it will actually escalate the situation if you quickly give "3 strikes" one after the other. Always restart fresh the next day whenever possible, letting them have a fresh start with "no strikes." It's important to state that for some children, allowing "3 strikes" before they are given a consequence can actually be a bad idea. Some children can start to rely on the fact that they have "2 more strikes left" before they have to change their behavior. If this is the case, don't use this "3 strike rule." But let your child know "there will be no chances or warnings".

■ Time Out

The use of "time out" can be very effective with younger children from ages 3 to 10. The point of a "time out" is to stop an undesirable behavior and allow the child to separate themselves from the situation to think about what they did and for them to develop a plan of how to change their behavior for next time. If the child does something they shouldn't, the parent requires their child to go to a specific place in the house for 1-5 minutes. For younger kids (under 5-6), a minute or less is usually more than enough time. This place should be private and not public (like in front of the other siblings), so as to avoid shaming the child. It can be standing or sitting, it doesn't matter. While in this "time out" location, the child is required to sit quietly or the parent will say, "I'm not starting the time until you are quiet in the time out spot." Once the child is done with their "time out," they can return. At that point the parent has a discussion with their child, such as, "Do you know why you got a time out?" and, "What will you do next time so you don't get a time out?" Again, make sure there is a reward program in place to focus on positive behaviors and not just the time outs. A big reason "time outs" work, especially for ADHD kids, is that they are SO BORING for the child!

Conclusion:

Make sure that your interactions with your child aren't always about "Did you do this?" or "Why didn't you do that?" If talking about problem behaviors is all a child gets from their parent, that's all they will expect from their parent. Make sure to have regular talks and interactions with your child that have nothing to do with obligations or responsibilities. Ask them about the weather or politics, their friends and activities. Laugh and enjoy your time together. When problem behaviors have to be brought up, your child will understand that's not all that matters to you.

Setting up systems to change behavior takes a lot of work at first. But once the system is used regularly, children quickly start adapting to the system and start changing their behavior. Once this happens, it actually takes much less work from the parent. A parent can finally relax when their children are acting in desirable ways. When this happens, take some time for yourself, or get on the phone with a friend and say, "Hey, I just wanted to call because my children are behaving wonderfully and I have a few minutes to talk until they are not."

Setting Up
Success at School

YOUR CHILD SPENDS a lot of time at school. Since ADHD children typically struggle with school, it's critical that classroom time is set up in a way that allows them to be successful. This chapter offers suggestions on what can be done to ensure success at school.

Schedule a Meeting

As a parent, you will serve as your child's primary advocate. It is ultimately up to the parent to make sure their child receives the educational services they need and deserve. If your child has been struggling at school, schedule a meeting with school staff (teacher, counselor, principal). It's beneficial to have this meeting right before the school year starts or soon after. At the end of the school year, it's helpful to have another meeting to set things up for the next school year. It's important to keep notes to document the date and time of these meetings, who was in attendance, and what was addressed. Documentation will help if there is a need in the future to recall what happened in these meetings. There are four key points to address in your meeting to help your child build the skills needed to become more independent and successful with their schoolwork.

1. Make sure that the school staff attending the meeting know your child has an ADHD diagnosis, a disability interfering with their schooling. Schools often require some documentation from your family doctor stating your child has ADHD, because schools classify ADHD as a medical disability.

2. Develop and provide a handout with short bullet points listing your child's strengths, as well as their challenges. Make sure each staff member at the meeting gets a copy. In this handout, identify what motivates your child and how those motivators can be used to help at school and at home. For example, let the staff know that your child works twice as hard when they are rewarded with computer time or a favorite comic book. Parents know their child best and this summary can really help the staff work more effectively with your child, especially if they don't know your child yet.

3. Require the staff to review any pre-existing academic plans (such as the IEP or 504 plan, which is discussed later in this chapter). Unfortunately, it's not uncommon for staff to have not read over the existing plan. If there isn't a formal plan already in place, a plan must be developed to outline the primary needs and goals for your child. The focus should be on actions to take immediately, and what needs to happen in the long term. The plan must address learning, social, emotional and behavioral issues.

4. Identify which staff members will be responsible for the implementation and monitoring of the approved plan discussed at the meeting. Accountability is achieved by establishing a weekly check-in to assess the plan's success. For example, the teacher may email the parent each week to give an update on homework completion and the current grade in the class.

Knowing Your Child's Legal Rights at School

ADHD is considered a disability, therefore it's important for parents to know the legal rights of their ADHD child in school. The Americans with Disabilities Act (ADA) and Individuals with Disabilities Education Act (IDEA) state that schools are required by law to accommodate any student with a disability. Here are some key facts about your child's rights:

- Schools categorize ADHD as a "medical disability." Your school may require a doctor to fill out a form to verify your child's ADHD diagnosis. Your family doctor is likely already familiar with this form.

- Schools must actively identify, locate and evaluate all children with disabilities, regardless of the severity (this is called "child find"). If a school knows a child has a disability and ignores it, they may be breaking the law.

- Schools are required to place your child in the least restrictive educational setting possible. This means schools must do *all they can* to allow a child with a disability to be part of the same classes and activities as all the other students in the "regular" educational setting.

- Schools are required to pay for all education, assessments and services essential to accommodate the educational needs of a disabled child, at no cost to the family. This is part of what's called "free appropriate public education" or FAPE.

Requesting an IEP or 504 Plan

Sometimes students with ADHD need more help than a typical education system can offer. It's very common for a child with ADHD to also have a learning disability. If they do, it's important to find out what learning disability they have. Proper intervention comes from an accurate assessment. If your child continues to struggle in school and current strategies are not working, consider requesting an Individualized Education Plan (IEP) or 504 plan.

An IEP is a written, detailed legal assessment and intervention plan for children experiencing disabilities (such as ADHD). Qualifying for an IEP involves many different tests administered by the school, and the process usually takes 1-3 months. The results of these tests help parents and school staff to identify what learning problems or learning disabilities your child may have. If your child qualifies for an IEP, a detailed intervention plan will be developed by the parents and school staff—teachers, counselor, school social worker, school psychologist, nurse, and other support staff. Having an IEP often means the child will receive extra time with school staff, will be given extra resources, and will be given special accommodations to help them learn. Some parents worry that having an IEP means their child will be pulled away from their regular class all day long. If your child is able to learn in their current classroom with special accommodations, they have a right to stay in that classroom.

A 504 plan is an accommodation plan to help students with disabilities. Basically, it is a significantly condensed version of an IEP. The term "504" is used because the plan comes from Section 504 of the Americans with Disabilities Act. In a 504 plan, a detailed assessment is not given to your child. All that is required is documentation from a medical doctor that your child has ADHD (a disability) and agreement from both the school and parents that the ADHD is interfering with their education. A 504 plan can be implemented quickly (within days). Simple accommodations in the 504 plan can include allowing:

- Extra time on tests and quizzes
- Reduction of schoolwork sent home
- Preferential seating (such as the front of the class)

If your child already has a 504 plan and it doesn't seem to be working, it may just need to be modified. If modifying the 504 plan still doesn't help, request that your child be assessed for an IEP instead.

School Discipline

Discipline issues can greatly impact an ADHD child's attitude and ultimate success in school. There are laws written in the IDEA that protect a child from being disciplined for violating a school's code of conduct if the behaviors were related or caused by a child's disability; or the legal term, "a manifestation" of the child's disability. In order for a child to have these protections, the school must have knowledge of the child's disability. The school *can* remove a child with disabilities to an alternative setting or give suspension for no more than 10 school days. If the removal is more than 10 consecutive days or if the child has been removed for a series of days that equal more than 10 days in the same school year for similar behaviors, this can be considered a change of placement. If the removal has been more than 10 days (either in a row or over time during the school year) the school must have a team meeting, with the parents included, to determine if the child's violation of the school's conduct policy was "(1) caused by, or had direct substantial relationship to, the child's disability; or (2) if the conduct in question was the direct result of the LEA's failure to implement the IEP" (43CRF 300.530- Authority of school personnel). "LEA" stands for local education agency. If during this meeting, the team finds that the behavior was a result of the LEA's failure to implement the IEP, they must take "immediate steps to remedy those deficiencies" (43CRF 300.530). If the behavior is found to be a manifestation or caused by the child's disability, the IEP team must implement a functional behavior assessment and implement a new behavior plan (or modify an existing behavior plan) and "return the child to the placement from which the child was removed, unless the parent and the LEA agree to a change of placement as part of the modification of the behavior intervention plan." (43CRF 300.530 (f) (2). There are a few exceptions. The school does have the right to remove a child with disabilities, regardless of their disability, for no more than 45 school days for behaviors related to weapons, illegal drugs or serious bodily injury of another person.

In regard to the school notifying the parents:

"(h) *Notification.* On the date on which the decision is made to make a removal that constitutes a change of placement of a child with a disability because of a violation of a code of student conduct, the LEA must notify the parents of that decision, and provide the parents the procedural safeguards notice described in § 300.504." (43CRF 300.530).

These are just a few highlights of the law. It is advised that the parent consult or hire an attorney to advocate for the rights of their disabled child if there is ever a removal or change of placement related to their child's disability. ADHD is considered a disability and an ADHD child has special rights to protect them in public schools.

Requiring an Accepting, Knowledgeable and Supportive Teacher

It's important that the parent and child have a positive, harmonious relationship with the school. In order for that to be successful, it is critical that your child be placed with a teacher who is accepting, knowledgeable and supportive of students with an ADHD diagnosis. To make sure this happens, talk to the principal or school counselor before teachers are assigned for the next school year. Ask that your child be placed with a teacher who is known to work well with ADHD students. When the school year starts, get to know the teacher. Make sure to introduce yourself and maintain regular contact throughout the year. Let them know you welcome regular communication about your child's progress. Teachers usually appreciate this open communication with parents. Listen to what your child says about the teacher and regularly ask your child how things are going with their teacher. Teachers that demonstrate knowledge, acceptance and support of ADHD will:

- Focus on the student's strengths.
- Acknowledge and praise students regularly when doing well.
- Verbally communicate to the students with respect and kindness.
- Be flexible and adapt their way of teaching to work for your student and not get stuck in a "my way or no way" teaching style.
- Show tolerance and patience when working with students.

Indications the teacher isn't accepting, knowledgeable or supportive of ADHD may be apparent if the teacher:

- Uses interventions that shame, humiliate or embarrass their students (which should NEVER occur). This can be something like the teacher telling the class out loud, "Looks like somebody forgot their homework again."
- Relies excessively on punishment and not enough on positive reinforcement to change behavior (like regularly taking away recess).
- Is inflexible.
- Makes comments that show a misunderstanding of ADHD, such as, "They are choosing to fail," or "If they don't have their name on the paper, they get 0% credit."
- Shows little tolerance and is quick to voice anger and frustration.

Trust your gut when something doesn't seem right. Listen if your child regularly expresses concerns about how the teacher treats them. For example, your child may comment, "My teacher doesn't like me," "My teacher hates me," or "My teacher is mean to me." If you feel the concerns about your child's teacher are significant enough, consider taking the following steps:

- Try to settle your differences in the least threatening or confrontational manner. Talk to the teacher one-on-one. Teachers are usually very open to meeting with parents. They may be unaware of your concerns. When you talk with the teacher, you may even find that your child didn't give you the entire story. Often this first step leads to a workable solution. Establish a weekly accountability plan, typically through a weekly email message reviewing how the agreed-upon solution is working.

- If things are still not resolved, request another meeting that includes both the teacher and an administrator (like the school counselor or principal). If your child already has a 504 plan or IEP, request these plans be reviewed and modified if needed. If your child doesn't have an IEP or 504 plan, this would be a good time to request one.

- If there still isn't a resolution, schedule a meeting with the main school district director of special education.

- If meeting with the district director doesn't work, consider consulting with a disability law attorney to help you find a solution. If things get to this point, make sure you have thorough documentation of everything that has happened thus far and all the attempts you have made in trying to resolve the issues.

- As a temporary solution, you may choose to keep your child home until a resolution is found.

- If all else fails to resolve your issues, consider moving your child to a new school.

Bottom line—don't wait too long to intervene and find a solution. Trust your instinct if something doesn't seem right. Begin talking with school staff as soon as an issue comes up so you can find a resolution. If things aren't resolved, the emotional toll on your child can be high. You can't afford to have your child placed with a non-supportive teacher for an entire school year.

Improving Success in the Classroom

Sustaining a consistent work effort at school can be a challenge for most ADHD kids. They often spend 2-3 times more mental effort and time to simply stay on task compared to other students. This can lead to your child becoming worn out, exhausted and frustrated. Here are some suggestions to help your child sustain their work effort in class:

- *Allow Extra Time:* Since concentration problems cause tasks to take longer than with other kids, allowing extra time on schoolwork and tests can make a big difference.

- *Accept Late Homework:* Kids with ADHD struggle to get homework turned in on time. Find out if the teacher will allow late work to be turned in at full credit. Everyone should agree that turning in late homework would only be a temporary solution while your child adjusts to the work load. If your child begins to rely on the fact that "they can just turn it in late," request a meeting with the school and teacher to develop a better plan. Interventions should always work toward your child turning work in on time.

- *Allow Breaks:* It can be helpful to allow 30 seconds of "drifting off" for a quick mental break or a longer 5-10 minute "free time" break. Along those same lines, it's important for school staff to avoid taking away recess, as this time helps improve effort later and is a much needed break from work.

- *Do Homework at School:* Kids with ADHD are often much more successful at getting their homework done during school time. This can be a study hall, homework class, study skills class or after school homework club. For many kids, this accommodation dramatically improves their grades and it seems confusing why many schools aren't doing it! If they are allowed to do homework during school time, it's best to allow it at the end of the school day, after their work has been assigned. If it's at the start of the day, it actually encourages them to put off doing their work at home because they think "I'll just do it tomorrow morning before class." It's also important that this "homework time" be used for just that—homework. If it's being used for something else (like talking to friends), the parent needs to be notified right away, that same day the homework isn't being worked on.

- *Allow Movement:* Many kids with ADHD may have problems sustaining effort because they need to move around. If they have to sit perfectly still, it's harder for them to focus on their work. Children who are hyperactive will tap on their desk, talk excessively, make noises, chew on things, tip their chair and/ or get out of their seat. As long as it's not disruptive to others, the teacher can consider allowing and even encouraging your child to:
  - Rock or wiggle in their chair (with wiggle cushions)
  - Doodle on a paper while they listen to the teacher
  - Chew gum or have something to chew
  - Hold items in their hand, like a stress ball or Silly Putty. Get creative, like having rubber bands wrapped around a pencil to allow the child to move the rubber band up and down the pencil
  - Move around or go do some physical activity to burn off energy (like helping the teacher take something to the office)
  - Allow extra recess and/or exercise time if needed. Physical exercise helps reduce hyperactivity later
- *Make Work Stimulating:* Kids with ADHD are much more engaged and focused on their work if they are stimulated with the work. To keep things stimulating, it helps:

- If the teacher is excited and interested in the subject as well
- To use humor and jokes periodically
- To use learning games
- To use videos or movies
- To allow your child some say in what project, subject or book they want

• *Give Rewards:* Effort is improved when there is a reward offered when work is done. Examples include:

- Allowing game time or computer time
- Allowing free time
- Allowing extra recess

Conclusion:

When schooling matches up well with what your child is capable of doing, parents and teachers will quickly notice increased success with their ADHD child. Children often go from feeling discouraged and defeated, to feeling encouraged and successful. When they experience success at school, they start enjoying school more and will feel better about themselves.

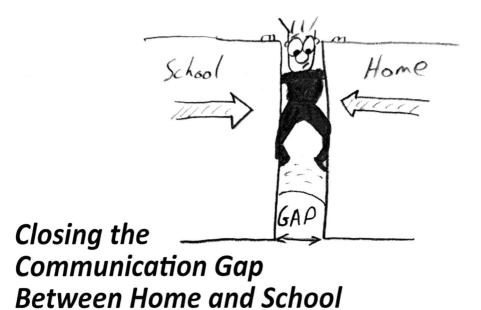

Closing the Communication Gap Between Home and School

ONE OF THE biggest factors that contributes to an ADHD child falling behind at school is the communication breakdown between school and home—teachers and parents. It is a major issue and can be a parent's greatest frustration. Building accurate and reliable communication strategies between home and school is a critical step in helping your child succeed.

Each day when your child returns home from school, a parent needs to know the following about their child:

1. Did they get to school and go to class on time?

2. Was their homework turned in on time?

3. Did they do well on their test or quiz?

4. Did they participate in class?

5. Were there any social or behavioral problems?

6. What schoolwork was assigned for that night?

7. Were the right materials for doing homework brought home (like books or worksheets)?

8. What projects, tests or quizzes are coming up?

9. What missing work needs to be completed?

For whatever reason, there seems to almost always be some sort of breakdown in communication between school and home. Parents inevitably throw up their hands and say, "I had no idea they had all this missing homework," or "I had no idea they were failing their tests." Relying solely on your child to accurately report what's going on doesn't work. And waiting until teacher / parent conferences or report cards is too late.

Building a sturdy bridge between home and school requires airtight communication between parents and school staff. Think of your child's school like a business where the managers are the parents and teachers, and the employee is the student. Like a business, how can there be success if the parent "manager" of one branch (home) and the teacher "manager" of the other branch (school) are unaware of what's going on in the other person's branch? It can't be successful. Or if it was somehow successful, they were just lucky.

A reliable communication system between school and home needs to allow:

- Teachers to report when all schoolwork is due (homework, tests, quizzes or projects) and gives enough time for you and your child to prepare for that due date.
- Teachers to immediately communicate to parents if schoolwork is not turned in on time.
- Parents and teachers to promptly report to each other when the child is struggling on specific work at home or in school.
- Parents and teachers to promptly report to each other when the child is showing concerns related to emotions (like crying in class or at home) or behavior (such as being disruptive to others in class).

At the beginning of the school year, talk with the teacher and agree to a communication plan that will be used for the rest of the year. It is best to examine the effectiveness of the school' existing communication system. Some or all of that system can be used. Whatever system is used, it needs to accurately report what happened at school *that same day*. It takes a lot of effort to keep this communication plan going all school year, so work hard to stay committed to it. Here are some tried and tested ideas that strengthen the bridge between school and home:

Use e-mail

Email is a quick and easy way for parents and teachers to communicate. Some teachers have been successful sending out emails to all parents, reminding them of upcoming due dates (like spelling tests). Parents love this! The teachers and parents need to commit to checking e-mail daily and responding to the e-mail within one day. Keep e-mails short and precise. If your child is struggling, request a daily or weekly email "check-in" until things improve.

Use the phone

It seems obvious to use the phone for communication, but teachers and parents are often hesitant to call each other. Phone calls can be the most time effective way to communicate and come up with solutions. It helps to keep calls shorter than 5 minutes.

Communicate face-to-face

Sometimes, when all other systems fail, the parent needs to communicate face-to-face with the teacher by scheduling a meeting. This takes more time to implement, especially when there are multiple teachers, but, when there is urgency it can be an effective, short-term solution. Make sure to create an agenda of what you want to address before the meeting.

Use the teacher's syllabus

The teacher can supply a class syllabus to the student and parent on the first week of school. A syllabus makes things easier for everyone and is highly recommended.

Use the school's online system

Many schools now offer a way to go online to check your child's academic progress. Many of these programs have the potential to report assigned homework, missing homework, absences, tardiness and current grades. The only problem is that these systems may not be completely reliable or timely. For example, a missing assignment may not be posted until two or more days after the due date. Your child can't afford to fall behind even by one day! If the online system works, then use it. If not, talk with the teacher to see if it's possible to make adjustments. If it still isn't working for you, something else needs to be used.

Use a traditional hand-written planner or an electronic device

As long as it's been proven to be accurate, use a paper planner or the planner in your child's smart phone or tablet to see what's going on at school. The use of planners is covered in more detail in the next chapter.

Conclusion:

It's extremely stressful and frustrating for parents to help manage their child's schooling when they don't have accurate information of what's actually going on at school. Parents are better able to help their child with school once an accurate and reliable communication system is set up between parents and the school. If a parent has to guess what's going on at school (with things like homework), or rely only on information given by their child, the chances of failure are much higher. Building an accurate and reliable communication plan between home and school is a critical step in helping your child succeed.

Starting and Finishing Schoolwork

STARTING HOMEWORK AND getting homework finished on time has proven to be one of the biggest challenges for ADHD children. From start to finish, homework requires a great deal of self-regulation and self-monitoring, which is a challenge for ADHD children. The reality is that parents and teachers will almost always need to step in and assist in some way.

Is getting homework done and studying for tests really that difficult? It only requires bringing the work home, doing the work and turning it in the next day, right? Unfortunately, it's not that simple. To get work turned in actually involves 32 steps (see Appendix A in the back of the book for a complete list).

If there are problems with homework completion or tests not being studied for, it's important to determine where the breakdown is happening. Here is a list of the skills needed to start and finish work on time:

- Recognizing (awareness that homework is being assigned)
- Understanding (what work needs to be done)
- Remembering (work needing to be done)
- Gathering (the work from the teacher and from home)
- Storing (securely putting work where it needs to go)

- Organizing (the work in a way that it can easily be found when needed)
- Bringing, Keeping and Retrieving (the work to home and back to school)
- Planning (the work that needs to be done and how it will be done)
- Starting (initiating work)
- Avoiding (distractions that will keep the work from being completed)
- Sustaining Effort (to finish the work and to keep continued work effort throughout the school year)
- Turning in Work

The process of doing work has a flow and a sequence. Each step is connected to the other. Miss one step, and the other steps are impacted. The goal is to identify which step(s) your child is having problems with. This chapter breaks down each of the steps and offers solutions to help get work done from start to finish.

Recognizing

Your child is certainly going to have problems with their homework if they didn't realize that they even had homework assigned to begin with. To get homework started and finished on time, the simple skill of awareness that homework has been given is obviously very important. That means your child needs to be listening and paying attention to what's going on throughout the class and to be alert when the teacher assigns homework.

SOLUTION: Make sure your child is physically placed in an area of the classroom where they can clearly see and hear the teacher, and the teacher can clearly see and hear your child. If your child is seated next to a student who regularly distracts them, consider moving your child to a seat away from the distraction. When homework or tests are announced, the teacher may need to do a quick check to make sure your child is aware of the assignment. For example, the teacher can look to see if your child was looking at them or that they are writing down the assignment as requested. If not, the teacher can prompt, "Write that down, please."

If this continues to be a problem, the teacher may need to check in after class to make sure the assignment was heard and written down. If that still doesn't help, it may be necessary for the teacher to have direct contact with the parent through email or phone to alert them of the homework or test that was assigned. The teacher can simply provide the student and parent with a syllabus listing what work is being assigned and when it's due.

Routine can also help the skill of recognizing. If homework or tests are assigned at the same time during class, students start to condition themselves to be more alert at that time to hear what's being assigned. Writing assignments in a familiar spot on the blackboard or whiteboard for the entire class may also be helpful.

Understanding

It's one thing to recognize that homework needs to be done, but it's another thing to accurately understand what and how it needs to be done. Getting the details of what work needs to be done is crucial. Some children arrive home knowing they have homework and turn it in the next day, only to realize they did it wrong (such as completing the wrong pages).

SOLUTION: If this is happening regularly, the teacher will need to check in with your child before they go home to make sure they understand what is being assigned. They can check the child's planner to verify the work was written down correctly. Again, the teacher can supply a syllabus to the student and parent which clearly states what needs to be done.

Remembering

The statement "I forgot" is all too common for ADHD kids. Of all the skills to get work started and finished, none are more important as the skill of remembering. Kids with ADHD have significant problems remembering, often because they are focused on something else at the time, or it's "out of sight, out of mind."

SOLUTION: The probability of remembering is significantly improved if schoolwork is handled the same way, every time, every day. Set a routine and sequence of how the work is done and where it's done, from start to finish. If your child forgets their schoolwork at school or home, the teacher and parent can help their child remember by requiring them to put their work away in their backpack at the same time and location every day. Reminders from the parent and teacher may be required until your child is consistent at remembering on their own. We all forget sometimes and your child will, too.

Reminder apps on smart phones have been a major help for people with ADHD. But obviously, your child must put the information into the phone in order to get the reminders and have the phone with them when the audio reminder alert goes off. Sometimes the parent needs to help schedule the reminders on the phone and remind them to have their phone with them.

Planners can also help remind your child what needs to be done and when things are due. Children with ADHD are often unsuccessful and/or unmotivated at using planners. Planners are discussed in more detail later in this chapter.

Sticky notes on computer screens, mirrors, walls or doors can also be helpful. These notes must be *noticeable*. For example, put the sticky note on your child's binder if they need to remember to ask the teacher a question. These reminders don't work as well if there are multiple sticky notes cluttered in one spot. They also aren't effective if it's the same sticky note every day, as kids get used to them being there and innocently don't notice them anymore. As with other reminders, if action isn't taken right away when the reminder note is noticed, there is a good chance the note will be forgotten.

Another great way of remembering items such as backpacks or paperwork is to place them in the same, easily noticed location every time. If your child is always driven to school in your car, why not just have them place their backpack in the car when they are done with their work the night before? Or if you always leave the house by the same door, you can place an item right beside the door, or hang it from the door handle so it's sure to be seen when you leave the house. Place the item somewhere you're sure to be and sure to see.

All these reminders work for your child, but will work for the parent as well. Many kids with ADHD have one or both parents who also have ADHD. It's hard to help your child remember, if you yourself forget things. Parents can use the skills listed above to help with remembering also.

Gathering, Organizing, Storing, Bringing, Keeping and Retrieving

These six steps are lumped into one category because they are closely related. So often, children with ADHD get home to do their work and realize they didn't bring the correct work materials home, or realize the next day that they didn't bring the correct work materials back to school. Gathering the correct work and work materials is a problem for most ADHD kids.

Just because the school items are "stored away," doesn't mean they will ever be found again or won't get lost. The word "abyss" comes to mind and is defined in the dictionary as "a deep, immeasurable space, gulf, or cavity; vast chasm." What better word to use to describe some ADHD kids' backpacks, lockers and work spaces? Kids with ADHD often will just throw their work into their binder, desk, locker or backpack with no thought of how they will find it later. When they get home that afternoon or back to school the next day, it has disappeared, never to be found again. This results in the work not being completed and not getting turned in on time. Schoolwork is often misplaced and or lost because there is no system or organization for where the work goes. Often the "system" being used is chaotic and scattered. Children will say their "system" works, but in reality it doesn't.

SOLUTION: When the work is assigned in class, it is very helpful if your child can be allowed to gather that assigned work and related materials right away and immediately place or store the work in an organized location (like a binder or backpack). Having a set time during the day when work is to be gathered also helps. If the correct work and materials are still not getting home or back to school, the teacher and parent will need to assist or verify your child has the right work and material before they leave school. Continue this until your child is able to successfully gather and prove they are reliable a bringing the correct items themselves.

All schoolwork, school materials and other school items need to be organized and kept in a secure location where it can easily be found and retrieved again when needed. To do this, all work and work materials need to be placed in the "right place" every time. I things aren't being put in the "right place," it's usually because there isn't a "right place" to put it. Make sure you buy your child every necessary item to store their school work and materials. If there are no places to put such items like pens/pencils, make sure to buy a pen/pencil holder that fits in the binder. If there isn't enough room for class notes and handouts in the current binder, stop using just one binder and get two binders instead. Desks and lockers should have places to store things neatly as well. Backpacks shouldn't have holes in them and lockers need to shut and lock completely (if it's broken, get it fixed). Make sure each school item has a secure place to go, where it can't get lost.

Store homework in a special "homework" folder, that has two pockets. On one side of the folder, write "to do" and on the other side write "done". This folder can be placed in their binder or by itself in their backpack. When homework is handed out, your child must immediately place it in the "to do" pocket (the teacher may need to prompt your child). They can even rip out a piece of paper, write down the assignment and place it in the "to do" pocket to remind them what work they need to do. This is an alternative when they aren't doing well by using the planner to write down their work. When all homework is complete at home, make sure your child places it in the "done" side of the homework folder. The teacher and/or parent may need to help to make sure this happens.

Make sure your child keeps a clutter-free and organized desk, locker, backpack, binder and folder. Put old schoolwork that can't be thrown away in another binder labeled "keep," away from their current work. This work can later be filed in a folder at home. Throw things that are trash in the *actual trash* (not the backpack). It's very common for kids to rip out notebook paper without opening up their binder first, causing rips in the 3 holes, and making it impossible to put back in the 3-ring binder. If that's the case, get those donut ring stickers to fix those ripped holes and place it in the binder where it belongs. Keep your child's backpack clean. If your child's backpack starts harboring fruit flies, it's time to clean it out!

Bottom line—keep things neat and in their designated place so everything can be easily found. Keep the *unnecessary stuff* away from the *necessary stuff*. Keep the system of organization as simple and clean as possible. Try to keep school items in one location.

Planning

Kids with ADHD would rather "do" than "plan to do." Planning takes time, it's not fun or exciting, and they would rather just "go for it." Many ADHD kids resist writing things down, choosing instead to keep everything "in their mind." They end up having problems keeping it all straight. Without proper planning, they don't get their work in on time and they don't prepare well enough for their tests or quizzes.

SOLUTION: To help keep all the schoolwork and due dates straight, it's helpful for your child to use a planner. Most of the time, ADHD kids hate using planners (or planning in general, for that matter). But, the planner is a crucial tool to help them become more independent with their work. The planner can either be a paper book-type planner or an app on your child's smart phone or tablet. The planner should be used to keep track of homework due dates, projects and tests. It also is a good place to write a "to do" task list for the day. If there are problems using the planner, the teacher will need to supervise the planner's use during school and make sure it's taken home. If your child is unreliable at bringing their planner home to you for review, the teacher may need to give you the work assignments and due dates directly (through email or at the start of each quarter). This accommodation may only be needed for one month. As mentioned earlier in the book, the teacher can supply the parent with their syllabus if they have one.

Note: For younger children (early elementary school), help them learn to use a planner by regularly writing down their school work and due dates on a white board or paper. They will become accustomed to seeing assignments written down, which prepares them for using a planner later.

When ADHD kids come home from school, they often don't have a plan for getting work done that night. They often put it off or think, "I'll have time to get this done if I start later," when in reality they won't have enough time or enough mental energy left "later." Remember, ADHD kids have problems seeing all the steps involved in doing a task and often misjudge how long a task will take. If they are experiencing problems managing their work, here is what you can do to help:

- Help them make a task list of all the work that needs to be done that night. Writing down everything makes things more concrete and helps an ADHD child physically see what needs to be done. The more concrete things are, the better they are at keeping it organized and prioritized in their mind. Writing it down also helps calm overwhelmed feelings. The written task list should be taken from your child's completed planner, their homework "to do" folder, or from the information you received from the teacher. Although you can write the homework task list on a blank piece of paper, some kids do better when it's written down on a large whiteboard.

- Place the task list where it can easily be seen and noticed. Write down all the homework and makeup work that needs to be done, as well as all tests and quizzes.

- Write down due dates for future assignments coming up, so they can visually see and prepare for them.

- Try not to add new tasks without warning. Nobody likes it when more work is assigned that they didn't anticipate.

When they get the idea of how to plan their work, start letting them develop and write down a list without your help (once they prove they can do it themselves).

Starting Schoolwork at Home

Just getting started on schoolwork is typically the most challenging part of getting work done. Your child will say, "I'll do it later," or "Let me finish this first." When your child is at home, there are SO many fun ways to avoid doing work. They may even decide that polishing the silverware is more fun than starting their math homework.

SOLUTION: Work before play is key here. It's challenging to start work when you are having a lot of fun doing something else. It is very important to require that work be started at the same time every day. Having a regular set time to start work greatly reduces the "fight" in starting the schoolwork and improves the chances of it actually getting done. Your child will be less frustrated if they already anticipate and expect when they need to start their work. If they start without prompting, that's amazing! If they need reminders, give pre-warnings of 10-15 minutes before work needs to be started. Many children do well with a timer as the prompter. Reward them when they start their work on time, and give an extra reward if they start without any prompting.

When prompting your child to start their work, try to talk minimally and calmly. Prolonged prompting is experienced as "nagging." Before starting these tasks, talk with your child about how you will "kindly help them get started by reminding them." Be clear that when the "kind prompting" is ignored, privileges or rewards will be lost. Periodically review how the routine is working and make changes when needed. Sometimes your child may want to try a different starting time. If they prove it works, allow it. But let them know if it doesn't work, you get to decide when work is started.

Avoiding Distractions

Once schoolwork has been started, getting distracted is common. The work either takes two to three times as long, or the work doesn't get done at all.

SOLUTION: Work should be done in the same location, where there is little or no distraction. It should be comfortable, free of clutter, provide good lighting and have all the tools needed to work (like a pencil sharpener or calculator). Make this workplace a *nice place* to work. Make it a special place, perhaps with a new chair they like, or getting a really cool desk lamp. We all work better in a place we find "special."

Be aware of what could cause distractions for your child and do what you can to eliminate those distractions from this area. Ideas to help get rid of distractions:

- Headphones to block out noise
- Workspace that looks toward the wall
- Work in a quiet area
- Parents not talking to their child or requesting things

Most of the time, eliminating visual and audio stimulus helps reduce distraction. However, there are some ADHD kids that can stay on task better when listening to music. The music itself helps them block out other distractions.

Sustaining Effort for Homework

Kids with ADHD have to use 2-3 times more mental effort throughout the day to stay on task and get their work done. This causes mental fatigue to set in.

SOLUTION:

- **Allow a break:** Breaks can include stimulating activities like video games or TV time, but be careful because sometimes breaks make it hard for the child to get started on their work. If they take a break right after school but then fight starting their homework, they lose their 30 minute break the next day and should be required to start their work as soon as they get home. They can earn that break time back the next day if they prove they can start their work without a fight.

- **Work in segments:** Set up short work periods (30 minutes) when longer work times are required, and allow short breaks (5 to 7 minutes) after they have worked for a specific time. If they aren't working during the study time, simply say, "I've stopped the timer," and don't allow a break until they reach the end of the agreed upon work period. Or instead of a timer, agree on how much work needs to be completed and allow a break after that work is done.

- **Reduce homework load:** Children with ADHD typically are taxed out mentally and exhausted after a full day of school. Adding a full load of homework that night may be unrealistic. For some kids it may be necessary to reduce the homework load. If you are finding your child is too overloaded with homework and having nightly "breakdowns" at home (showing increasing levels of depression, anxiety or defiance), it's time to talk with the teacher and school to figure out what can be done and develop solutions. Again, pushing a child beyond what they are capable of doing will not work. It may only be necessary to reduce the amount of homework required by the school for a short period of time (like one week). Or a plan could be made where the child does no more than 45-60 minutes of work per night. The parent can monitor this time to make sure they are actually working and not messing around.

- **Try it their way:** Your child may have their own ideas of how they can best get work done. Make a rule of "let's try it" and evaluate if your child's idea works. For example, if they think listening to music while they work will help, maybe it will. If it seems reasonable, give it a try. But if it doesn't work, let it be known that the parent gets to decide how the work will be done next time.

- **Give rewards or privileges:** Give rewards or allow privileges only after work is done.

- **Sleep:** Sleep is often overlooked. Sleep is very important for good mental function and sustaining effort. Be sure sleep is adequate (at least 10 to 11 hours for elementary and 8-9 hours for teens). Some children have sleep disorders and are not rested even after adequate sleep time. Talk to your doctor if you have concerns about your child's quality of sleep. Resolving sleep issues can have a dramatic effect on better focus and self-regulation.

- **Avoid activity overload:** Kids sometimes just have too many activities planned. Don't over-do it! Remember that your child is exerting more mental energy than most just to maintain an appearance of normalcy. We live in a society of "GO, GO, GO! You can do more." But sometimes we just need to say, "NO, NO, NO! I need a break!" Going beyond our human capacity will never work. Being "out of gas" and out of mental energy will result in not being able to sustain effort on work.

- **Encourage healthy eating:** From sugar to dyes in food, there are many who question what effects these have on ADHD children. Regardless of proof, it's safe to say that a healthy diet of fruits, veggies, whole grains and protein, as well as drinking enough water (not soda) can have a positive effect on an ADHD child (and any child for that matter). Talk with your doctor about your child's diet. When the brain is given all the nutrients and energy it needs, sustained effort is greatly enhanced.

- **Stay encouraging and positive:** Staying positive will help you AND your child to stay on task. A good rule is for every one corrective comment, there needs to be three positive comments. Communicate with a caring and supportive attitude. Don't forget to laugh and use humor. Most parents would agree that laughing together with their child is one of life's best treasures. It's much easier to keep working when you are in a good mood, and that goes for children, too.

- **Exercise:** It has been proven that exercise helps with mood, sleep, concentration, stress and an overall feeling of well-being. All of these help with sustained effort. If your child isn't getting enough exercise, find ways to keep your child physically active. This can include sports, riding bike, or taking hikes.

Turning In Work

When school work is completed and brought back to school, it then needs to be turned in. Sounds simple, right? Unfortunately, this last crucial step can be missed and some kids will spend hours on their homework, only to forget about turning it in the next day.

SOLUTION: Remembering when and where to turn in work is obviously very important. If your child is not remembering to turn in their work, there is nothing wrong with the teacher announcing in class "OK class, turn your homework in." It's also helpful if the teacher has a regular routine where work is turned in at the same time and location every day. If the homework still isn't being turned in, develop a plan to have the teacher verbally prompt your child to turn in their work until your child starts turning it in independently.

Conclusion:

Getting work completed from start to finish involves many more steps than one would think. Being aware of these steps allows teachers and parents to figure out exactly where the breakdown is happening and to develop solutions to address the problem. Once these issues with homework are figured out and resolved, grades will often dramatically improve.

Starting and Finishing Home Responsibilities

THE PREVIOUS CHAPTER focused on the steps required for starting and finishing schoolwork, but non-school tasks at home, such as chores, require the same steps.

Recognizing and Understanding

Kids with ADHD often don't recognize when their parents are assigning a task. Even when they do, there is often a problem where they quickly assume they "know what needs to be done" and don't listen for the details of what *actually* needs to be done. For example, the parent may say to their child, "I need you to take out the trash to the street before going to school this morning." Not hearing a response, the parent realizes their child wasn't listening to them and has to repeat the request. Stated a second time, the child hears their parent, but only hears "take out the trash" and in their mind say "yep...got it." Unfortunately, the child incorrectly assumes the parent wanted the trash taken from the kitchen to the trash can in the garage. As a result, the trash can is not taken to the street as requested.

SOLUTION: Your child needs to be aware a task is being assigned and understand what needs to be done. Many kids with ADHD don't like their parents verbally telling them what to do. It often works better for the requested tasks to be written down instead. It's helpful to have a routine time and place where the written tasks are assigned, such as having the daily tasks listed on the whiteboard by 7 a.m. As soon as your child gets up in the morning, they will know what is expected of them that day. Parents need to use this routine every day, otherwise the child will not be motivated to check the whiteboard.

A great way to make sure tasks are done correctly is to make a checklist of the task requirements. If the task "clean your room" is never completed correctly, make a "cleaning your room checklist" that details each required task to clean the room, such as "make your bed, put dirty clothes in hamper, put clean clothes in drawer, vacuum floor, etc." Put this checklist on paper and attach it to a clipboard. Require your child to check off each item as they go. This can be more time consuming for the parent at first, so type it out and save the check list on the computer. That way it can be printed and used again. With a detailed checklist to complete a specific task, the job that needs to get done is rarely misunderstood.

Remembering

Just like school work, remembering what tasks or jobs need to be done is a significant problem for ADHD children. If it's out of sight, it's out of mind. The parent may request that their child put their clean clothes away before bedtime. After school their child sees their clothes and thinks to themselves, "I don't want to do it now. I'll do it later tonight." They truly intend to do it later. However, that night when it's time for bed, they walk into their room and see their clothes still on the bed and say, "Oh man, I forgot to put my clothes away. I'm too tired. I'll do it tomorrow." Unfortunately, "I'll do it tomorrow" can last a week or more.

SOLUTION: Like we discussed in the school section, setting up reminders on a cell phone or on paper are helpful. But reminder usually will only work if the task is done right away. As your ADHD child gets older, it's important for them to learn a statement they can say in their mind, and that is, "If I don't do it right now, I probably will forget, or won't do it at all."

Planning

Kids with ADHD are horrible at planning on getting their work done and frequently underestimate how long work will take. They often take on or plan more activities than is realistic or humanly possible. As a result, they either rush to get their work finished on time or the work doesn't get done at all.

SOLUTION: When planning tasks, a thought that is very helpful for people with ADHD to keep in mind is, "You do not have nearly as much time to get these tasks done as you may think." Just like with schoolwork, it helps tremendously to write down each item on paper or a whiteboard to have a visual. Write down the estimated time it will take for each task. This will help prioritize what needs to get done first. Make sure to overestimate how long each task will take, so as to allow extra time if needed. Ideally, your child will see the benefit of doing this type of planning and start doing it independently.

Gathering, Storing, Organizing, Bringing, Keeping and Retrieving

Again, these steps are lumped into one category because they are closely related for completing tasks at home. To get the job done right, you need the correct tools or materials and the ability to promptly find those items when needed. Kids with ADHD often lose things and will place items in the most random places, making them hard to find.

SOLUTION: Every item or tool necessary to do a task needs to have "their place" and be put back in "their place" when the task is finished. If the item doesn't have a place, then make a place or go buy a place for the item. For example, buying a simple wall holder clip for the broom and dustpan and requiring them to always be put back in that same place can ensure they will be easily found when needed. If an item is discovered out of place, require your child to take the item and put it in its correct location.

Having containers to store work items is helpful. For example, a tote used to keep all the bathroom cleaning tools can help ensure the items don't get lost and are put back where they belong. Having a tote also saves time collecting items needed for a task and helps with bringing the items to the task location (such as the bathroom). It's also important that occasional effort is spent de-cluttering so work items aren't buried beneath a heap of trash, never to be found.

Starting, Avoiding Distractions, Sustaining Effort, and Finishing Work

It's so easy to be at home and avoid starting and finishing chores and obligations. It's common to think, "This will take too long," or "I'll do it later after I have a little fun." Kids with ADHD have problems transitioning from stimulating, fun activities to less stimulating activity such as chores.

SOLUTION: Just like with school work, the old saying "work before play" applies here too. Require that work is done before your child is allowed to "play." Make a set routine when work is required to be started and stick to this start time as much as possible. This can be a specific time on the clock, or after a specific activity (like after eating breakfast). Have rewards set up when work is completed.

When work is being done, try to eliminate things that can distract from work, such as turning off or putting away the cell phone. Work can be made more enjoyable by allowing such things as playing music, as long as it doesn't interfere with work getting done.

In order to get a task done right away, people with ADHD usually have to fight the thought that the task "will take too long," or take time away from something else they want to do instead. But in reality, the task usually doesn't take that long at all (making a bed takes less than 1 minute). Starting a task often requires confronting the "this will take too long" thoughts.

Routine, Routine, Routine

With all the steps required to start and finish a task, it can't be stated enough (so it will be stated again) how important and helpful it is for ADHD children to have daily and regular routines in their lives, both at home and at school. Doing things the same way, every day, greatly improves the chances that schoolwork and home tasks will be started and finished successfully. Routine is one of the most important ADHD strategies for parents and teachers.

Conclusion

There are many steps required in getting work done at home, at school or on the job. When work is not getting done, evaluate where the breakdown is happening—which step or steps are causing difficulties. Once the problem is found, it often only takes a few adjustments to get work completion back on track.

Handling Anger

ANGER IS A normal emotion. Levels of anger can shift throughout the day depending on what's going on. When a child's anger starts to escalate, they usually find a way to calm those emotions themselves, without adult help. But there are times when a child's anger escalation doesn't stop and reaches a point of no return. Let's call this the "freak out stage." In that stage, a child may cry, yell, go silent or act aggressively toward themselves or others. During a "freak out," a child will react with more of an animalistic-like reflex and will likely do or say things they will regret. Some kids get to the "freak out stage" very quickly like a light switch and others are more tolerant and have a slower anger escalation.

Adults can be pushed to high levels of anger as well, even to the point of their own "freak out." As a parent or teacher, there will be many times your tolerance will be tested and pushed to the limit. Just like with a child, when anger levels get too high, adults also tend to make poor choices and say things they shouldn't.

Managing your own anger and helping your child manage their anger is important. Here are some helpful ways to manage anger:

1. Be Aware of the Intensity of Anger

Calm < 1 - 2 - 3 - 4 - 5 - 6 - 7 - 8 - 9 - 10 > *Angry*

Using a 1-10 scale (like the picture above), help your child learn that there are different levels or intensity of anger. Point out how everyone gets angry and that it's normal. Have the child point to number 1 on the scale and tell you about a time that they remember being really calm. Help them out with some examples if they are unsure. Then point to number 10 and have them give some examples of when they were the angriest they have ever felt. Finally, have them give a few examples of times where they were somewhere in the middle, at about a 5. With children younger than 6-7 they may have trouble understanding the number scale. Instead of using numbers you can describe escalating anger as a balloon filling more and more with air. When the balloon is too full, it pops. Explain, "We want to stop the anger when the balloon is only half full to make sure to let some air out, so it doesn't pop".

2. Catch Escalating Anger Early

When anger gets too high (above a 5), we don't think as rationally and wind up making poor choices. We are better able to self-regulate our frustration when our anger is lower. When anger is noticeably escalating, don't ignore it. Address it early in the escalation process.

Escalating anger usually has a lot to do with a person being too rigid in a situation and not recognizing that the way they are trying to do things is not working. This happens to all of us. Things never go 100% as planned and the more adaptable we are, the less angry we will be. Think of possible ways you can make adjustments in that moment, instead of pushing forward in a way that isn't working. Take 3-5 deep breaths to re-group and calm yourself. Teach your child how to do the same when they feel angry. Calmly talk about the situation that is creating the escalation in anger and see if there are possible solutions to resolve it. If anger continues to escalate to higher levels, go to the next step (step 3).

3. Take a Break When Anger Escalates Too High

Take a mutually agreed upon break when frustration gets too high, like anger that gets higher than a 5 on the scale. For example, you can have a pre-made plan with your child that "when voices start to rise, that means we are probably getting to a 5 or higher. Let's make a deal to take a quick 5-minute break from each other when that happens." Often, when things start to escalate, it's best to physically get away from each other for a few minutes. It's almost impossible to de-escalate if whatever is causing the anger continues. When anger levels get too high, a person is really in crisis and this is NOT the time to continue talking. If your child refuses to leave, then you leave. Make sure that leaving was already discussed and is part of the plan. Make sure you both agree to leave respectfully. This means neither the parent nor child will say anything to get a "last word" or do things like slam a door to the bedroom. When leaving, use tact and say calmly, "Let's take just a 5-minute break and come back to this." Keep in mind that the child can also request a "5-minute break" when they see you as the parent getting too angry. This isn't just one sided.

4. When Anger Settles Down, Try Again

Agree to "try again" when you both think your frustration has lowered and you both are willing to talk together respectfully and peacefully. When it's time to return to your child, hear them out and let them talk first. Validate their emotion. This doesn't mean you have to justify or agree with their emotion, but only understand where they are coming from. The parent can then share their feelings. This is a good time to figure out what each of you is wanting from the other and to see if you can come up with a working solution for both of you. If things got out of hand, this is a good time to apologize and say "I'm sorry." If needed, the parent may need to start with their own apology first.

Many times when the parent and child get angry with each other, it is helpful to work together to find an agreeable solution. This may include making some compromises together. But there are also times when a parent needs to set the rules firmly, where there is no compromising or negotiating. If a parent gives in too often when their child gets angry, it can actually lead to the child using their anger to get what they want. The child learned that anger "worked." When your child gets angry and you need to hold your ground, managing your own anger and staying calm is important. This is a challenge for any parent. A parent staying calm, even when their child's anger is escalating, is a great role model for good anger management skills. In cases like this, set the rule and stand firm.

Conclusion:

Remember, anger is normal. Never miss this point. Anger itself doesn't cause problems. It's the way the anger is handled or allowed to get out of control that can create problems. Monitoring anger levels and catching escalating anger early is the key to effectively managing anger for yourself and your child.

Medication

DECIDING WHETHER OR not to put your child on ADHD medication is a difficult decision. Understandably, people feel uncomfortable and resistant about giving their child a pill for ADHD. But in truth, medication can be helpful and even life changing for some people living with ADHD. Most would agree that medication should not be the first strategy used for an ADHD child. It's important to first start with non-medication strategies. There are many non-medication suggestions given in this book. Also, medications should never be the *only* strategy. Medication should only be used in conjunction with behavioral interventions.

When a parent is considering putting their child on ADHD medication, it's helpful to use a cost/benefit assessment of the situation. Make a list of the "cost" of not starting the medication, and a list of the "benefits" of starting the medication. Basically, a parent needs to ask the question, "Is there more harm in not starting them on medication?"

Example 1: A child in 4th grade has had continued problems with learning their math. In addition to ADHD, this child has a math learning disability. Even with special education services, this child still has problems paying attention to their teacher during math class and staying focused on their math assignments. Even with special education services to give more one-on-one math instruction, the child is falling more and more behind. This child is also becoming more depressed about their lack of success and has started to cry in math class.

The inability to keep attention is likely a significant factor in this example. Using ADHD medications *could* help. With declining math performance and increasing emotional distress, the parent may feel that things have gotten to the point that *not* trying the medication is maybe causing more harm than giving medication a try.

Example 2: An 8-year-old girl continues getting in trouble with her teacher for "causing disruptions" during class. She has a history of being much more hyperactive and energetic than her peers, tipping her chair or tapping her pencil on her desk. Even though she finds it hard to sit still during class, she *is* still listening, paying attention and learning. When class is more interactive and engaging, she is less hyperactive and more calm. This is especially true when the learning requires getting up and physically moving around (like going outside to look at different trees for science). So far, there have not been any special behavioral plans made to help with these "disruptions" in class. In this case, before starting medication, it would be a better idea for the parent and school staff to meet together to develop a behavioral plan. The fact that she is still paying attention and learning is a positive. Is medication really needed? Non-medication strategies mentioned in this book (such as allowing movement in class) would be a better starting point for her. Making sure the teacher is accepting and familiar with educating children with ADHD is crucial. Having the child start medication to simply "make her less disruptive" would be inappropriate.

When considering ADHD medications, it's important that the parent choose a professional who is knowledgeable and up-to-date with the current ADHD assessment and intervention strategies.

Prescribing doctors and providers should be diligent when prescribing ADHD medications to children. If they are diligent, they will:

- Require that a thorough assessment be done to verify the child has ADHD.
- Rule out other social, mental or physical issues that might be affecting the child at home and school.
- Ask the parent what non-medication strategies are already being used, and not prescribe ADHD medications until there is evidence that non-medication strategies were tried first.
- Require behavioral interventions in addition to the child taking the ADHD medications.
- Refer the family to a behavioral therapist that specializes in childhood ADHD.

Conclusion

The decision to start or not start a child on ADHD medication is the parent's choice. If a parent would rather not start medication, that decision should be respected and supported. The parent should not feel forced by others to put their child on medication. But if a parent *does* start their child on medication, this should also be respected. Medications, along with behavioral interventions, have helped many ADHD children find success.

Conclusion

THE NUMBER ONE job a parent has is… well, to parent. But, what does it mean to "parent"? The dictionary.com site defines it as "the methods, techniques, etc., used or required in the rearing of children." In that definition, it's the "etc." that causes a parent the most challenges. And what does it mean to "rear" a child anyway? No, it doesn't refer to spanking and it can't simply just mean "to raise." Parenting is much more than that.

To parent means preparing your child for adulthood, so they can live independently. To parent means helping a child *live* their life, not just *survive* their life. To parent means teaching resilience and toughness. To parent means helping foster happiness and joy. To parent means giving of yourself, not giving for yourself. To parent means loving your child and letting them know why *they* should love who they are.

Parents will likely have some challenges with their ADHD child. Parenting takes a lot of effort and determination. Your child may only give you an online review of 3 out of 5 stars right now, which really isn't fair. But don't quit! (Like you have a choice anyway.) When they are older, they will see just how much work, effort and love you gave to them. Of course, once they realize this, make a big deal of it and be sure to say something like, "Thanks for noticing, that means a lot… it was worth every minute." But more importantly, make sure to get them to edit that online review to a 5 out of 5 stars… if they don't mind. You've earned it!

Steps to Get Schoolwork Done, From Start to Finish

REVIEW EACH STEP listed below with your child to pinpoint where the problem exists and take action to fix it.

During the School Day

1. Be present in class when work is assigned.

2. Be aware and alert that work is being assigned.

3. Listen and accurately identify what schoolwork needs to be done (homework, projects, tests/quizzes).

4. Listen and accurately identify when schoolwork is due.

5. Write in the planner what schoolwork needs to be done and when it's due.

6. Collect the assigned work materials (such as a worksheet that has been assigned).

7. Store the work materials where they will be remembered (backpack and binder).

8. Store the planner where it will be remembered (binder and backpack).

9. Bring the assigned work and materials with you at the end of class.

10. Store the binder and backpack in a place that it will be remembered and safe from being stolen or lost.

At the End of the School Day

11. Retrieve your backpack or binder to bring work home.

12. Identify what work needs to be brought home (from the work written in the planner).

13. Gather the appropriate schoolwork and work materials to bring home after school.

14. Store the schoolwork and work materials in a place that guarantees it will get home and be easily found, such as the backpack.

15. Take the backpack with you and keep it with you until you get home.

At Home

16. Bring the backpack and work materials to your workspace (like the desk).

17. Take the planner and homework out of your backpack and review the work that needs to get done that night.

18. Develop a plan on how and when the work will get done that night.

19. Write down a task list, making sure to prioritize what work needs to get done first.

20. Get started on the work.

21. Sustain effort for the amount of time needed to get the work done thoroughly.

22. Review the completed work for accuracy and quality (such as name on the paper, or to make sure it is complete).

23. Cross the finished work off the task list.

24. Place the finished work in the binder and backpack.

25. Place the backpack in an area where it will be remembered tomorrow morning.

The Following Day

26. Remember to get the backpack and take it with you to school.

27. Keep your backpack with you until you get to school.

28. Store the backpack and the finished work in a safe and secure area at school where you can retrieve it when needed (in locker).

29. Remember what work needs to be turned in at a class, before going to that class.

30. Gather and bring that completed work to class.

31. Listen for the teacher's instructions on when and where to turn in the finished work.

32. Follow through on the teacher's request and turn in the finished work in the location and the time the teacher instructed.

APPENDIX B

Worksheet: Understanding Behavior Outcomes

What did you do?

Why did you do that? (What was your intention?)

What did the other person think and feel about what you did?

What did the other person do next? How did they respond?

Did your behavior work like you wanted? Like you intended?
(What worked? What didn't?)

5

What could you have done differently that might have worked better?

6

How will your behavior effect the relationship in the future?

7

APPENDIX C

Worksheet: Understanding the Behavior and Intent of Others

What did the other person do?

Why do you think they did that? (What was their intent?)

What did you think and feel about what they did?

What did you do next? How did you respond or react?

Did their behavior work as they intended?
(What worked? What didn't?)

What could they have done that might have worked better?

Was there a misunderstanding? Did you misjudge their intent?

CPSIA information can be obtained
at www.ICGtesting.com
Printed in the USA
FSOW02n1711150117
29506FS